WEST VIRGINIA
GETAWAYS

WEST VIRGINIA
GETAWAYS

A GUIDE TO THE STATE'S

BED
& BREAKFASTS
AND
COUNTRY INNS

EDITED BY
QUARRIER PRESS · CHARLESTON, WV

Quarrier Press
Charleston, West Virginia 25301

© 1999 by Quarrier Press.

Book and cover design: Mark S. Phillips, Marketing+Design Group

First Edition, First Printing
Printed in Canada

Library of Congress Number: 99-65780
ISBN 1-891852-08-6

TABLE OF CONTENTS

ACKNOWLEDGMENTS

The publishers would like to thank all of the innkeepers and others who provided information for this book. We greatly appreciate the hospitality of those innkeepers who provided us with food and lodging while we traveled throughout the state. A very special thanks goes to Colleen Anderson, Douglas Imbrogno, Lauren Kline, and Mark Sadd for their assistance.

INTRODUCTION

West Virginia differs from most states, especially those on the East Coast, by its pristine beauty and relatively small population base. Rough and dramatic terrain, with mountains and rivers and gorges, have played the largest part in preserving the natural beauty and small town feeling found throughout most of the state. West Virginia's history is a colorful one, beginning with its formation by secession from Virginia at the outset of the Civil War. This long and vibrant history, coupled with its topography, persons with foresight, and some luck, have all resulted in the state retaining many well-preserved historic districts and buildings. Luckily for prospective travelers, this has resulted in a relatively large number of charming bed & breakfasts and inns in the state, many located in handsome historic properties. *West Virginia Getaways* will help the interested traveler find a great place to stay, while enjoying the unique beauty, history, and recreational opportunities of the Mountain State.

This book primarily covers the historic bed & breakfasts and inns of West Virginia. However, in our effort to offer interesting lodging options in all regions of the state, we have also included many special cottages, modern homes, and camp- and farm-like settings, which do not fall into either the B & B or the inn category. We have included these because they are charming and offer a welcome respite from the corporate sameness found in many hotels and motels.

For purposes of this book, we have broken down the state into eight separate regions: the Eastern Panhandle, the Monongahela Forest, the New River and Greenbrier Valley, the Morgantown Corridor, the Coalfields, the Metro Valley, the Ohio Valley, and the Northern Panhandle. The Eastern Panhandle contains over a third of the B & B entries in this book. Other regions have as few as two or three entries. Within each regional breakdown you'll find the names of the towns containing B & B's in that region. The B & B's are then listed alphabetically by town, and within each town, alphabetically by the name of the establishment.

We have tried to apply a consistent approach in reviewing each establishment. For each entry, we have tried to provide an illustration; a general description; directions on getting there; the innkeeper's name; address and telephone; web page and e-mail if applicable; number of rooms; prices; pet, children, and smoking policies; and special features and attractions at the inn and in the area.

Every establishment in this book requests that guests make reservations in advance. When you call to make reservations, please verify the price and the directions, and any policy which you think will have a bearing on your visit. While many B & B's welcome children, many do not, or are not set up to accommodate them. If you are traveling with children, discuss their ages and needs with the proprietor beforehand. Likewise if you are traveling with a pet. While the majority of B & B's do not permit smoking indoors, most permit it outdoors on the porches or property. Check with your host.

This book is by no means a complete listing of every B & B and inn in the state, but it is a pretty good start. While we did attempt to visit as many B & B's as possible, we could not visit all of them. Changes, and changes of ownership, may be par for the course.

We hope that this book will help you to enjoy your travels in West Virginia. You will discover many treasures if you follow the leads in this book. We hope that you have as much fun visiting these B & B's as we did!

THE STAFF OF QUARRIER PRESS

EASTERN PANHANDLE

Berkeley Springs, Charles Town, Gerrardstown, Great Cacapon, Harpers Ferry, Hedgesville, Martinsburg, Paw Paw, Romney, Shepherdstown

About the region . . .

The beautiful Eastern Panhandle of West Virginia is an important spot geographically. Sitting strategically midst three states, with the Shenandoah Valley to the south, the area saw and suffered many pains and glories during the Civil War. In an earlier era, George Washington surveyed the region, and fell in love with it. Eventually many of his relatives settled in the Panhandle. Today the region is revered by natives as well as Washingtonians, who frequently travel the short distance from D.C. for weekend getaways. Some residents of the Panhandle commute daily to Washington. The area becomes more of a "suburb" of our nation's capitol every day, albeit with important, and wonderful, differences. Among them, that about eighty per cent of the region's land is used for agricultural purposes. Given this fact, most of the area's rolling hills, farmland, and rivers remain relatively pristine. As do the historic districts and houses which survived the ravages of the Civil War, many of them now offering respite as treasured landmarks and bed & breakfasts.

The large number of bed & breakfasts in the Eastern Panhandle is reflected in this book; over a third of the entries herein are in the Eastern Panhandle. The largest towns in this region are Berkeley Springs, Charles Town, Harpers Ferry, Martinsburg and Shepherdstown. While most of the B & B's in the Panhandle are in one of these towns, some lie further out, in places with names like Paw Paw and Great Cacapon. Most of the outlying bed & breakfasts are close to one or more of the principal towns; the five towns themselves all being in close proximity to each other. For more information on the Eastern Panhandle, contact the Jefferson County Convention and Visitors' Bureau at 800-848-TOUR or 304-535-2627; Travel Berkeley Springs at 800-447-8797; or the Martinsburg Convention and Visitors' Bureau at 800-4 WVA-FUN.

The town of **Berkeley Springs**, originally known as Bath, was named for the warm mineral springs that bubble up from the mountains in the center of town. For generations people have traveled great distances to bathe in these healing mineral waters: George Washington frequently bathed in the springs for their health benefits. Berkeley Springs boasts ten B & B's, two antique malls, great shops, restaurants, and The Star movie theater, home to overstuffed couches and an old-fashioned popcorn machine.

The nearby town of **Charles Town** dates to 1786, when Colonel Charles Washington, George Washington's younger brother, provided eighty acres for the establishment of the town. By then young George

Washington had already invested in 550 acres of land along nearby Bullskin Run. While visiting and traveling through the town, you will see many streets named for the Washington family. Charles Town sits among the foothills of the Blue Ridge Mountains, and is home to the Charles Town Races, the Jefferson County Museum, and the Old Opera House. The town made history when it became the site of the famous trial and hanging of abolitionist John Brown.

A visit to historic **Harpers Ferry** is a must. The town has a breathtaking view of Maryland, Virginia, and West Virginia, as well as the magnificent confluence of the Potomac and Shenandoah Rivers. Connecting Harpers Ferry and Washington, D.C. is the ever popular C&O Canal Towpath, frequented by bikers and hikers. Most of the town is a national park, and it draws about half a million visitors each year. The town is named for Robert Harper, a gentleman who operated a ferry service across the rivers in the mid 1700s. During the Civil War, Harpers Ferry changed hands eight times, causing it to suffer great damage. The National Park Service has restored much of the town and its buildings. Constantly undergoing reconstruction, Harpers Ferry offers a picturesque and accurate look at the times of John Brown and his contemporaries.

Berkeley County was created in 1772 by the Virginia Assembly, with **Martinsburg** being named the county seat. However, its first permanent settler is recorded living here as early as 1729. The town of Martinsburg was laid out on 130 acres of land owned by General

Adam Stephen. Stephen named the town for his good friend, Thomas Bryan Martin. Martinsburg had significantly divided loyalties during the Civil War, sending soldiers to fight for both the North and the South.

Perched on the banks of the Potomac River, **Shepherdstown** was laid out in 1734 by Thomas Shepherd. The town is considered by many to be the oldest in the state. Because of its strategic location on the Potomac and its proximity to the C & O Canal, it prospered until the Civil War. Today it is home to the growing Shepherd College, circa 1871. The College, its students, and faculty, all add to the vivacity, charm, and cultural offerings of Shepherdstown.

BERKELEY SPRINGS

Aaron's Acre Bed & Breakfast

Situated on a hill above historic Berkeley Springs is a charming re-stored farmhouse, Aaron's Acre Bed & Breakfast. Its wraparound porch offers guests a perfect place to unwind, while affording a prime view of the sunset behind Warm Springs Ridge. Your hosts Zora and George Payne have turned this 1920s farmhouse into a delightful, elegant, and welcome place for visitors. We entered the house through a door into the dining room, where we immediately spied a wonderful antique farm table. Guests eat breakfast at this table, which was lovingly crafted of wood salvaged from an old barn. Guests will enjoy the adjoining living room, which features board games for relaxing and boasts exquisite woodwork.

The two guest rooms in the main house are on the second floor. The first, the Lace Room, has a gorgeous antique queen size bed and private bath. The second room, the Rose Room, also has a private bath, and an antique queen size bed. All the guests rooms are especially clean and elegant; each is furnished with beautiful linens and unique beds. The next two guest rooms are located in an outbuilding called the Carriage House. The first is decorated in a masculine palette, with hunter green walls and plaid linens. This room has a lovely wood and iron queen size bed, private bath, and private entrance. The second guest room has lovely pine paneling, a queen size bed, full kitchen, and private bath. It also has a private entrance, as well as its own private deck overlooking the hills of Berkeley Springs.

Guests at Aaron's Acre will enjoy the quiet hospitality of Zora and George Payne. Their elegant furnishings and obvious attention to detail add to the enjoyment of their guests. Located a few streets away from downtown Berkeley Springs, Aaron's Acre is worth seeking out (there is no sign downtown to advertise it.)

How to get there: From I-70, take Route 522 South (Washington Street) through Berkeley Springs. Go through all three traffic lights in town. At the next intersection, turn left (left turn only) onto Johnson Mill Road. Aaron's Acre is the 7th house on the right.

Innkeepers: Zora and George Payne

Address/Telephone: 501 Johnson Mill Road, Berkeley Springs, WV 25411, 304-258-4079.

Web page: www.berkeleysprings.com/aaron/index/htm

Rooms: 2 in main house, each with private bath. Carriage house has 2 bedrooms, each with private entrance and bath. Sorry, no children under 12, pets or smoking.

Rates. From $ 80. - 105., double occupancy. Special rates for extended and mid-week stays. Reservations required. Accept Mastercard, Visa, personal check, cash.

Open: Year around.

Facilities and activities: Nearby are Berkeley Springs State Park, Cacapon State Park, fishing, hiking, tennis, Robert Trent Jones golf course, cross-country skiing, horseback riding, paddle boats, and swimming. Also nearby are outlet malls, antique and craft shops, and auctions and flea markets. Of course, the springs, baths and massage in Berkeley Springs are the destinations of many.

The Barn

"The Barn" bed and breakfast is an old barn which has been converted into a comfortable, furnished house for week or weekend getaways. Situated on 31 acres of farm and forest land, the Barn offers a peaceful respite midst natural beauty. The house is charming, retaining the exposed oak beams and tin roof of the original structure. Spacious windows and a large deck offer wonderful views of the valleys and adjacent mountains. The Barn sleeps up to ten people, has a modern bathroom and fully equipped kitchen. A wood burning stove, electric heat, and ventilation fans assure your comfort year around.

There is a llama farm behind the Barn — a short 15 minute walk away. Biking and exploring are available in the woods of the property's 31 acres. Relax on the large deck and enjoy views of beautiful valleys and two mountain ranges.

How to get there: From I-70, take Route 522 South going through Berkeley Springs. Go 2 miles past town and turn left on Route 13 (Old Winchester Grade Road). Go 2.5 miles, take a left at Spriggs Road across from a one-lane bridge. Go .5 mile up to the second place on the right; the white barn is visible from the roadway.

Innkeeper: Pat Spranger

Address/Telephone: (owner) 204 Parkside Road, Silver Spring, Maryland, 20910. (301) 587-5495.

E-mail: pspranger@aol.com

Rooms: Converted barn is rented as a unit. Has large living room, kitchen, laundry room, bathroom. One bedroom has a king size bed and a double bed. There are 2 lofts, one of which sleeps 3 and one 4. Children welcome; pets allowed with a small fee.

Rates. $ 185. for 2 for a weekend; $ 385 for 2 people for a week; price increases with more guests. Call for reservations. Cash or personal check welcome.

Open: All year.

Facilities and activities: Nearby Berkeley Springs offers spas with soothing mineral baths and massage. Local artisans and collectors display their treasures in quaint shops and antique stores. Outdoor activities in the area include hiking, horseback riding, tennis, golf, swimming, and cycling.

The Country Inn

Offering the amenities of a large hotel with the charm of a small inn – that's Berkeley Springs' The Country Inn. The Inn was built in 1932, and sits on the original site of the old Strother Hotel, which burnt down in 1898. The Inn's motto is "Retaining the Best of the Past." The colorful colonial history of the town is linked to the Inn; among the original lot owners of the property were three signers of the Declaration of Independence, as well as George Washington.

While staying at The Country Inn, guests may enjoy the Inn's spa with trained masseuses, or the refreshing mineral baths next door at the state park. The Inn also has a gift shop, a large formal restaurant, and lovely gardens for strolling. Be sure to visit the Inn's art gallery, which has an organ and a piano.

Thirty of the 67 guest rooms are in the original part of the Inn; 37 rooms have been added in a new building behind the Inn. Most of the guest rooms have private baths; a few have a shared bath in the hall. Each room in the Inn is decorated in a unique manner, and no two guest rooms are exactly alike. There are several smoking guest rooms available. The Inn has a large conference room which is available for business meetings.

Since the Inn is conveniently located in downtown Berkeley Springs, its guests can easily visit the town's shops, restaurants, theaters, and churches.

How to get there: From I-70, take Route 522 South, which is Washington Street, into Berkeley Springs. The Inn is located on the right at 207 South Washington Street.

Innkeepers: Alice Barker

Address/Telephone: 207 South Washington Street, Berkeley Springs, WV 25411, 304-258-2210/800-822-6630, fax 304-258-3986.

Web page: www.countryinnwv.com

E-mail: countryn@intrepid.net

Rooms: 67, some with private bath. Nine smoking rooms available. Children welcome, but no pets allowed. Smoking in specified areas only.

Rates: $ 40. - 136. per night. Minimum stay is two nights on weekends from spring through November 1. Accept Mastercard, Visa, American Express, Discover, personal check, cash.

Open: Year around.

Facilities and activities: In-house spa with whirlpool, gift shop, restaurant, and gardens. Next door is Berkeley Springs State Park with baths, spa, and massage. Former Lawrence Welk Show performer Tom Wetherton is a regular draw at the Inn.

Folkestone Bed & Breakfast

Folkestone was built by Captain L.H. Kirby in 1929. The second owners of the property, the Hawkins, named the ten acre estate "Folkestone" after their home in England. Jennie and Walter Harmison purchased Folkestone in 1942. The Harmisons also operated the prestigious Country Inn in Berkeley Springs. Famous persons who came to Berkeley Springs and wanted more privacy than was afforded at the Inn often were housed at Folkestone. Hence, such prominent guests as Alice Roosevelt Longsworth, Vice President Alben Barclay, Cardinal Cushing, and John L. Lewis have all stayed at Folkestone.

The present owner, Hettie Hawvermale, inherited the property in 1969. Hettie is an interesting and welcoming host, and will put you at ease immediately. If you like dogs, you'll find that Hettie's dog Missy is one of the friendliest around. The lovely wooded grounds at Folkestone reflect the best of its English heritage and its natural country setting. Guests enjoy leisurely walks among dogwood, azalea, oak, forsythia, rhododendron, roses, and other beautiful plants and flowers. You might like to try a long hot soak in the deep Japanese soaking tub. At cocktail time, Hettie likes to serve guests cordials with fruit, cheese, and crackers.

Guests can choose from one of two bedrooms in the main house, or rent both as a suite. Since there is just one bath, Hettie does not rent both rooms unless the parties are together. Therefore, guests will have a private bath unless they are traveling with friends. There is a cozy sitting area between the rooms, with a small refrigerator for guests' use. The small bedroom has an antique four poster bed and Hettie's inkwell collection. The large bedroom is spacious, with a sitting area overlooking the woods.

While in the upstairs common sitting room, look for a specific album which contains fascinating newspaper stories about the Folkestone ghost! While the ghost, or ghosts, have been gone for years, local townspeople, and Hettie, enjoy talking about the strange goings-on. Hettie recalls the ghosts as friendly and mischievious. Often she would run upstairs to check on footsteps heard from below, only to find no explainable source. One time when preparing for guests, all her silver teaspoons disappeared, only to reappear shortly thereafter. For whatever reason, the ghosts seem to have left Folkestone for other accommodations.

Breakfast is served either in the dining room, which has lovely stained glass windows, or, weather permitting, on the screened porch, which is surrounded by rhododendron. Breakfast includes juice, fresh fruit, homemade pastry or breads, a daily entree and coffee, tea, or milk. Special dietary requests can be accommodated, but should be made one week in advance.

How to get there: From I-70, take Exit 1B, house is 1.5 miles east of Berkeley Springs on Rt. 9. Also located only 6 miles from Hancock, Maryland.

Innkeeper: Hettie Hawvermale

Address/Telephone: Rt. 7, Box 13740, Berkeley Springs, WV 25411, 304-258-3743.

Rooms: 2, with a shared bath for groups or private bath for one couple. Smoking tolerated. Sorry, no pets or children under 15.

Rates. $ 80. for two persons. Includes breakfast and some special dinners. Accept personal check or cash.

Open: All year.

Facilities and activities: With 24 hours notice will have Japanese hot tub available in spring, summer, and fall for $ 10. per evening. Enjoy historic Berkeley Springs and visit the Spa, the Castle, local museum, antique shops and restaurants. Also nearby are golf, boating, fishing, horseback riding and hiking.

The Gamekeeper's Cottage

Return to days gone by and spend a weekend in the charming 200 year old log cabin that is the Gamekeeper's Cottage. Your hosts, Jean and Jeff Thatcher, live in a home across the meadow from the cottage, and look forward to having you. The rustic luxury of the Gamekeeper's Cottage is guaranteed to offer you a rejuvenating week or weekend.

Days at the Gamekeeper's Cottage are full of fun things to help you unwind. The old fashioned front porch overlooks a private pond, and you can fish in adjacent Sleepy Creek. Guests can also use the dock and rowboat. You may want to explore — on foot or bike — the lovely meadows and woodlands surrounding the property, or relax on the porch with a view of Sleepy Creek Mountain. You can bird-watch and see other wildlife without leaving this quaint country lane. In cool weather, the abundant woodpile makes it easy to get cozy in front of the living room wood stove. In warm weather, you will sleep comfortably in your air conditioned bedroom.

The Gamekeeper's Cottage has three bedrooms. Downstairs is one small bedroom with a double bed. Also downstairs is the bathroom, with its charming claw-foot tub (with shower) and pretty linens. Jean enjoys putting fresh flowers in the rooms as often as possible. Upstairs is a beautiful pine bed, heaped high with comforters and pillows. The third bedroom has a twin bed, desk, and small television. The cottage also has a television and VCR downstairs, as well as a telephone. The full kitchen is well-stocked with breakfast makings, gourmet coffee and tea, a microwave, dishwasher, and cooking necessities.

Should you choose to tear yourself away from your beautiful surroundings and cozy accommodations, nearby Berkeley Springs offers plenty to do. In addition to shopping, restaurants, and mineral springs, the Thatchers claim that Berkeley Springs boasts more massage therapists than attorneys. I'd say that's a pretty good selling point for Berkeley Springs.

How to get there: From the stoplight at the intersection of Route 9 East and 522, travel 2.5 miles east on Route 9. Turn right on Peter Yost Road and go exactly 2 miles to a 3-way stop sign. Bear right at the stop sign and travel .7 mile down a steep hill. At .7 mile, the road will curve sharply to the right, but a small one-lane private road marked "Do Not Enter" goes straight. Take this road. The 4th house on the left belongs to your hosts, the Thatcher family. Check in here. The 5th house on the left is the Gamekeeper's Cottage.

Innkeepers: Jean and Jeff Thatcher

Address/Telephone: Route 2, Box 156, Berkeley Springs, WV 25411, 304-258-1375, fax 304-258-4524.

Web page: www.berkeleysprings.com/gamekeepers/ or www.virtualcities.com

E-mail: jthatch@ix.netcom.com

Rooms: 3 bedroom cottage, one private bath. Children welcome; well-mannered pets accepted by prior arrangement and advance deposit. Sorry, no smoking inside.

Rates: $135. per night, $ 750. per week; sleeps 5 to 7 persons. Includes provisions for self-made breakfast. Call for weekly and week day specials. Reservations recommended and deposit required. Accept cash or check.

Open: All year.

Facilities and activities: Nearby are hiking and biking trails, cross country skiing, horseback riding, and fishing. In Berkeley Springs are historic baths and massage treatments; unique shops and galleries; fine dining and antiques. The Cottage is 15 minutes from 2 premier golf courses.

The Glens Country Estate

Travel down a particular country road, and you'll soon happen upon the lovely house and grounds that comprise the Glens Country Estate. From the road, you can see the inn's large white porch, with its inviting ceiling fans and rockers. Approaching the house you'll pass a stream, with some ducks lazing away the day. Sitting on thirteen acres, the house is a beautifully restored Victorian treasure, with almost every modern amenity.

Guests enter the Glens through the large foyer, which has high ceilings and skylights; it is very bright and airy. Off the foyer guests will see the large dining room. If you take a peek out back, you'll spot the inn's large luxurious in-ground pool out back. Plenty of comfortable lounge furniture had me longing to relax pool side.

A specialty of the Glens are its candlelit, six course gourmet dinners served on china and crystal. After a perfect meal, guests will want to retire to their comfortable oversized bedrooms with king size beds, cable television, and private bath with jacuzzi. Guests are served breakfast in the privacy of their own rooms.

The original part of the house is what was once called a "Sears Roebuck House." These were houses that were ordered from Sears Roebuck: the materials came in the mail with directions for putting a house together. This house was renovated about seven years ago, and the owner lives on the premises. Originally there was no indoor plumbing. Subsequently, all the pipes were added outside the house.

The Glens has two certified massage therapists on call by appointment. There are also more than 500 tapes in the video library. The Glens also restored and rents an 1878 house called the Glens Victorian House, which lies 3 miles from the main estate. Smaller and more private, it has many amenities of the main house. Guests at the Victorian House can also use the massage facility, pool, and (with reservations) enjoy dinner at the main house.

How to get there: Call for directions.

Address/Telephone: Route 2, Box 83, Berkeley Springs, 304-258-4536/ 800-984-5367.

Web page: www.wvglens.com

Rooms: 11, all with private bath. Sorry, no pets or children. Absolutely no smoking on the property.

Rates: Owners request that you call for rates. Room includes full breakfast served in your room; lunch and dinner are available by reservation. Reservations are suggested two to three months in advance. Pay half in advance by check; all credit cards accepted at check-in.

Open: Year around.

Facilities and activities: Two certified massage therapists available on site with appointment. Jacuzzis, in-ground pool, television, video library. Close to historic Berkeley Springs, with mineral baths, the Star Theater, and nearby state parks.

Highlawn Inn

Slip into the past with the charming setting at Highlawn Inn. Highlawn was built in the late 1890s by the Honorable Algernon R. Unger for his bride, Chaffie Ziler. Unger served in the West Virginia legislature and built the landmark Washington Hotel — which was destroyed by fire in 1974 — in Berkeley Springs. After his death, his widow began operating Highlawn as a boarding house. The current owners bought the house in 1984, meticulously restoring it to its original elegance. The main house is a Victorian charmer, boasting a wraparound verandah with a premiere view of the spa town below.

There are six charming bedrooms to choose from in the main house. All contain eclectic antiques, and have lovely, golden pine floors. Guests enjoy relaxing outside on the inviting antique glider or on sloping lawns criss-crossed with pebble paths and filled with flower and herb gardens. If you look out by the bird bath, you're likely to see one of Sandra's three cats patiently awaiting a feathered visitor. The cats live in the main house and love guests. For those not feline-inclined, however, try one of the other three cat-free buildings on the properties.

A popular option at Highlawn for those seeking very private quarters is to rent the Carriage House. Here, the loft of the original carriage house has been converted into a huge living space with a high peaked ceiling and exposed beams. The Carriage House has unique offerings such as a whirlpool bath behind French doors, triangular windows, stained glass and a library nook. Guests love the electronic remote that ignites a gas fireplace at the foot of the bed. Original cedar siding and sunlight wrap the room in a warm glow. Curl up on the couch in front of the fire, and enjoy a movie or get ready to nod off. Many guests staying in this special place never want to leave it. Actually, it is sometimes referred to as "The Lover's Loft," as at least four marriage proposals have taken place here!

The third option at Highlawn is to stay in the charming cottage called "Aunt Pearl's", which is just a footpath away from the main house, nestled among Aunt Pearl's beloved gardens. There are four Victorian guest rooms in the cottage. A tiny pantry in the rear is always open for tea, coffee, and Berkeley Springs mineral water. While taking the pebble path to the cottage, look for one of the cats curled up under a bush, or sunning its stomach.

The fourth option is "The Bathkeeper's Quarters", which rents to one or two couples in the same party. Guests enjoy the privacy of their own porch and views, but can walk around the corner to eat in the dining room at the main house. The Bathkeeper's Quarters has a front and rear parlor, a large whirlpool room, a well-appointed kitchen, two private baths and two lovely bedrooms with antique beds.

Innkeeper Sandra Kauffman displays immense talent and energy running this ambitious establishment. Whether welcoming guests returning from a walk with her fresh-baked pastries, decorating the house with beautiful flowers, or preparing sumptuous meals, Sandra clearly enjoys the hospitality business. The menu from her Easter dinner left my mouth watering, and my delicious breakfast at Highlawn included lemon poppy seed cake with fresh mint. The breakfast was served on antique dishes, all decorated with her nasturtiums, pansies, and herbs. Starting the day at Highlawn is a real pleasure.

How to get there: Route 522, which runs through Berkeley Springs as Washington Street, is accessible by I-70, 81, and 66. Follow Route 522 either north from Winchester, Virginia, or south from Hancock, Maryland (exit 1B off I-70) to Market Street and Route 522. Follow the street two blocks to the top of the hill. Highlawn is on the left.

Innkeeper: Sandra Kauffman

Address/Telephone: 304 Market Street, Berkeley Springs, WV 25411, 304-258-5700/888-290-4163.

Web page: www.virtualcities.com/ons/wv/p/wvp4601.htm

Rooms: 12, all with private bath and color television, some with VCR and movie library. Sorry, no pets; children allowed over age 14. Smoking is allowed in some rooms.

Rates: $ 85. - 185., double occupancy. Full breakfast included. Dinners available May through October and all holidays. Discounts for extended stays. Accept Visa, Mastercard, personal checks, and cash.

Open: All year, except December 24 through December 26.

Facilities and activities: A wealth of activities are available just an easy stroll down the hill. Bathe in historic warm mineral springs, yield to the relaxing fingers of a massage therapist, hike nearby mountains, or treasure hunt at local antique shops.

The Manor Inn

Travel up the shady drive of The Manor Inn and park under the huge shade trees. The Manor Inn is nestled on a hillside two blocks from the center of historic Berkeley Springs. The Inn is a second Empire Victorian with a large wraparound front porch. It was built in 1874 as the home for the mayor of Bath, Alexander T. Sloat. Special features of the house include twelve foot ceilings, French doors to the front porch, and a shingled mansard roof. The Inn has recently been restored, and is listed on the National Register of Historic Homes. While staying at the Manor Inn, sit and rock on the broad Victorian porch with a cool drink in warm weather, or curl up in front of a fire in the parlor when the weather is cool.

The interior of the house is decorated with antiques, crafts, and beautiful quilts. Your host's collection contains about ten turn-of-the-century quilts, most of which are in perfect condition. Many other newer quilts are the handiwork of Donald's deceased wife

Dottie, who was a talented quilter. To find out which quilt graces your guest room, climb the majestic curved staircase to the second floor. Each of the four guest rooms features a comfortable queen size bed. If the activities in Berkeley Springs wear you out during the day, curl up with one of 130 movies in Mr. Trask's video library. Enjoy your stay at the Manor Inn, a very charming place.

How to get there: From I-70, take Exit 1B, go south on Rt. 522, at the second traffic light turn left. The Manor Inn is the 6th house on the right.

Innkeeper: Donald Trask

Address/Telephone: 415 Fairfax Street, Berkeley Springs, WV 25411, 304-258-1552.

Rooms: 4 bedrooms, one with private bath, one with shared bath, one 2 bedroom suite with private whirlpool bath. Sorry, no smoking, pets, or children under 10.

Rates: $ 85. - 180., includes full breakfast. Check, Mastercard, Visa, and cash accepted. Check out at 12:00 noon.

Open: All year.

Facilities and activities: Horseback riding at nearby private and public stables; swimming at Berkeley Springs and Cacapon State Parks; golf, tennis, and hiking nearby. Shopping at Blue Ridge and London

Fog Outlet Centers. Movie fans will enjoy the local Star Theater, which shows the latest movies Friday through Sunday nights at old fashioned prices. For only .50 cents extra you can reserve a sofa for your movie watching. The house overlooks the springs and state park.

On the Banks Guest House

Guests at On the Banks Guesthouse are sure to enjoy its fun atmosphere and friendly, outgoing hostess, Mary Banks Nichols. On the Banks is an 1875 Victorian home situated on a hill overlooking scenic Berkeley Springs. A doctor built the house after the Civil War for use as a summer home for his family. Mary Banks Nichol's grandfather bought the house for her parents as a wedding present in 1929. It has remained in her family ever since.

The house has two regular bedrooms for guests, and a big sleeping porch with two double beds for use when large groups visit. The porch is both screened and glassed in. If the weather gets extra warm, it can be air conditioned. The two regular upstairs bedrooms share two bathrooms; one bath is upstairs and one is downstairs. The Marie Antoinette Room has a king size bed and a walk-in closet. The second bedroom has a queen size bed and pretty wicker furniture. The guest rooms have air conditioning, fireplaces, and telephones.

Guests will want to explore and enjoy the many other elegant rooms of the house, most of which are filled with artwork and curios Mary has brought back from her many travels. Enjoy the baby grand in the Music Room, or the fireplace and gaming table in the library. Guests are served a full breakfast in the formal dining room. Your hostess will accommodate specific dietary restrictions and requests if given sufficient notice. Mary enjoys using fresh produce from her kitchen garden, and likes to cook with an international flair.

Your hostess, who is a lot of fun, says the house has a "No smoking, no streaking policy." Guests often enjoy sitting on the large front porch, enjoying a view of the town, or playing checkers with Mary.

How to get there: Berkeley Springs is readily accessible from Interstates 70, 81, and 66 at the junction of U.S. 522 and State Route 9. Follow Route 522 either north from Winchester, VA or south from Hancock, MD to Martinsburg Road (Route 9E) in Berkeley Springs (look for a Sheetz convenience store on the corner). Follow Martinsburg Road to the first bend in the road. On the Banks Guesthouse is at 304 Martinsburg Road.

Innkeeper: Mary Banks Nichols

Address/Telephone: 304 Martinsburg Road, Berkeley Springs, WV 25411, 304-258-2134, fax 304-258-8441.

Web page: www.berkeleyspring.com/banksguesthouse/

Rooms: 2, with 2 shared baths. A group can rent 4 bedrooms and share 2 baths. Sorry, no smoking or pets. Children welcome.

Rates: $ 80. - 85. per night; group rates available. Request half payment deposit. Accept check or cash.

Open: Year around.

Facilities and activities: The house is located close to Berkeley Springs, so visitors can take advantage of boating, canoeing, swimming, fishing, and horseback riding. Visit Berkeley Castle, Cacapon State Park, Paw Paw Tunnel or Prospect Peak. In town, enjoy shopping, restaurants, massage therapists, mineral springs, and tennis or golf.

Sunset Mountain Farm

Sunset Mountain Farm is a great house for one or two couples or a large family who want a private country getaway. The house itself is located on a beautiful 40 acre farm. Guests will enjoy the rustic stone fireplace, original hardwood floors, and the gorgeous sunsets. The house has two bedrooms, a full bath, a fully equipped kitchen, dining area, and living room. Outside there is a wonderful deck overlooking the pond and picturesque mountain views. For the year around comfort of guests, there is a wood burning stone fireplace in the living room, as well as central heat and ceiling fans.

While staying at Sunset Mountain Farm, guests enjoy a variety of activities, including exploring the property on hikes or on bikes, fishing and swimming in the pond, or cooking great meals in the kitchen. Perhaps the most popular activities are just watching the sunset, taking a nap midst the quiet landscape, or snuggling on the sofa with a good movie. For those craving a little more activity, the town of Berkeley Springs is just 20 scenic minutes away.

How to get there: Owners request guests call for directions.

Innkeeper: Sandy Kay

Address/Telephone: P. O. Box 323, Berkeley Springs, WV 25411, 304-258-4239, fax 304-258-4653.

Rooms: 2 bedroom house with full bath and kitchen. Well-behaved pets and children are welcome. Prefer non-smoking guests.

Rates: $ 125. daily double occupancy; $ 15. each additional person; weekly rates available. Deposits required; Mastercard, Visa, and checks accepted.

Open: Year around.

Facilities and activities: Enjoy 40 rolling acres with fishing, biking, swimming, hiking, or cross country skiing. Located near Cacapon State Park and Sleepy Creek Lake & State Forest. In downtown historic Berkeley Springs you'll find its mineral baths, massages, antique shops, and restaurants.

CHARLES TOWN

The Carriage Inn

The Carriage Inn is a grand colonial home, built in 1836 on a shady acre facing East Washington Street. The home is known by Civil War historians as the site of a strategy meeting between Generals Ulysses S. Grant and Philip Sheridan. Guests approach the Inn across a spacious lawn and move to the inviting front porch. The home has been carefully and faithfully restored, and is decorated to reflect its original era.

Each of the five guest rooms have a private bath and a queen size four-poster bed. The rooms are spacious and comfortable and furnished with period antiques. Four of the guest rooms have working fireplaces. A delicious hot breakfast is served in the "East Parlor." Guests enjoy perusing Civil War mementos and books located in the West Parlor, and are invited to share the Inn's board games, television, and refrigerator. The Carriage House was opened for guests in the summer of 1997. It has a three-room suite with private bath, and is the perfect place for a family with young children.

Your hosts, Al and Kay Standish, look forward to your visit and will be happy to make suggestions for sight seeing or other activities. They can also give interested parties historical information on the house and the town. The Carriage Inn offers birthday, anniversary or get away weekend packages, which are great gift ideas.

How to get there: From Virginia, take Route 7 west to the junction with Route 9, 4.5 miles west of Leesburg. Follow signs for Charles Town through Hillsboro and across the Shenandoah River. Upon entering Charles Town, continue straight on George Street. Go to the second traffic light, turn right onto East Washington. After four blocks you will pass the Inn; turn right on Seminary Street. From Maryland, take I-70 West to a junction with US 340 South near Frederick. Cross the Potomac into Virginia, continue on US 340 through Harpers Ferry about six miles to a junction with Route 51 at the eastern edge of Charles Town. (Do not take the Route 9/340 bypass.) Go straight down East Washington past the Charles Town Races; turn left on Seminary Street.

Innkeepers: Al and Kay Standish

Address/Telephone: 417 East Washington Street, Charles Town, WV 25414-1077, 304-728-8003/800-867-9830, fax 304-728-2976.

Web page: www.carriageinn.com

E-mail: innkeepers@carriageinn.net

Rooms: 4, plus one suite in main house, all with private bath. The Carriage House features a 3 room suite with private bath. Sorry, no smoking or pets. Children over 10 welcome in main house; Carriage House can accommodate 2 younger children with responsible adults. Check out is 11 a.m.

Rates: $ 75. - 95. weekday; $ 115. - 135. weekend and holiday. Includes full gourmet breakfast. 10% discount for stays of three nights or longer. Lunch or dinner du jour available on request for additional charge. Accept Mastercard, Visa, cash or check.

Open: All year.

Facilities and activities: Enjoy the porch swing, board games, or croquet on the premises. The house is Stop No. 9 on the walking tour of Charles Town. Guests can walk to the site of the John Brown trial and the gallows; antique shops, and live theater at the Old Opera House. In the area are several Washington family estates, as well as outlet shopping, golf, and white water rafting.

The Cottonwood Inn

The Cottonwood Inn is nestled among the rolling farmland of the Shenandoah Valley. You approach the 150 year old Inn by crossing a small bridge over Bullskin Run. The Cottonwood is located on six acres, and guests frequently comment on its peace and privacy. Visitors enjoy exploring the property, looking for birds and wildlife. You may want to take a picnic lunch to the outdoor pavilion, or stay on the front porch, taking in the view from your comfortable rocking chair. If the weather drives you inside, there is an extensive library. You'll also find videos on driving trips in Europe, produced by hosts Joe and Barbara Sobol.

The interior of the house has colonial decor, furnished with antiques, reproductions, and quilts. All of the guest rooms have private baths, as well as four-poster queen size beds. While Colonial in era and decor, the house does have air conditioning for hot days, as well as comfortable sitting areas with fireplaces for when the temperatures fall. The Cottonwood Inn is a comfortable farmhouse in an inviting setting . . . come here to get away from it all.

How to get there: The Cottonwood Inn lies 6.5 miles south of Charles Town. From the center of Charles Town, take Route 9 for three miles to Kabletown Road. Turning right on Kabletown Road, you will be heading south. Travel 3.2 miles to Mill Lane. Turn right on Mill Lane, the Inn is .3 mile ahead.

Innkeepers: Joe and Barbara Sobol

Address/Telephone: Route 2, Box 61-S, Charles Town, WV 25414, 304-725-3371/800-868-1188, fax 304-728-4763..

Web page: www.mydestination.com/cottonwood

E-mail: travels@mydestination.com

Rooms: 7, all with private bath. Children welcome. Sorry, no smoking or pets. Check out time is 11 a.m.

Rates: $ 75. - 120. per night, includes full breakfast. Accept Visa, Mastercard, American Express, cash, or check. Midweek discounts available.

Open: Year around.

Facilities and activities: Six acres for exploring, outdoor picnic pavilion, video guides on European driving trips. Nearby are historic battlefields, antique shops, horse and car racing, outlet malls, golf, rafting and canoeing.

The Gilbert House

Take a step back in time and enjoy the warm hospitality of Bernie Heiler at the Gilbert House Bed & Breakfast. A private residence, the house was built around 1760, and is on the National Register of Historic Places. A grand stone house, Gilbert House is full of elegant rooms and tasteful antiques. Guests can enjoy the Georgian splendor of several bedrooms, each with private bath and air conditioning. Honeymooners or visitors looking for something special will want to stay in the unforgettable Bridal Suite.

Located in the quaint village of Middleway, one of West Virginia's oldest settlements, Gilbert House is located in the center of the Historic District. You may want to take a guided tour of this timeless village. While in the area, enjoy the beautiful scenery, canoeing, hiking, horse races, and antique shopping. Visitors at the Gilbert House will relish their host's gourmet breakfasts, often featuring eggs served with a steak or salmon fillet.

How to get there: Located six miles west of Charles Town, via WV 51. Travel south .5 mile on County Road #1. Guests will see sign for Middleway Historic District. Gilbert House is the large stone house with a small sign.

Innkeeper: Bernie Heiler

Address/Telephone: P. O. Box 1104, Charles Town, WV 25414, 304-725-0637.

Rooms: Several rooms, each with private bath; also have Bridal Suite. Sorry, no smoking or pets. Children welcome with responsible parents.

Rates. Start at $ 75. Includes full breakfast. Visa, Mastercard, and American Express accepted. Reservations required.

Open: All year.

Facilities and activities: Near historic Harpers Ferry and the Antietam Battlefield, the Gilbert House is located on the Settlers Trail into the Shenandoah Valley.

Hillbrook Inn

For travelers looking for a special place to stay for an important occasion or indulgent weekend, visit Hillbrook Inn. While guests here do get a "bed and a breakfast," Hillbrook Inn offers much more, and clients gladly pay for it. One of the main reasons guests come to Hillbrook Inn is for the work of the full-time chef, Christine Hale, who specializes in gourmet, seven course dinners and has been at Hillbrook for many years. Guests can elect not to eat the formal dinner ($ 70. a person), but most come with that particular indulgence in mind. Complimentary drinks are served in the afternoon, and a high English tea is served on Sundays for an additional charge. Clients not staying at the hotel may dine at Hillbrook for breakfast, lunch, or dinner. Reservations, of course, are required.

The other main attractions for guests at Hillbrook are its extraordinary setting and beautiful, sophisticated, yet comfortable, interiors. To reach Hillbrook Inn you turn at the sign and travel down a long gravel road, passing the owner's home on the right. Striking outcroppings of limestone fill the property. As you approach the large tudor mansion, you'll see a chess board on the lawn with chest high playing pieces. You travel over two lovely duck ponds filled with lily pads and water plants as you drive to the parking area. The house is approached by walking up a beautiful terraced garden, filled with a lion's head fountain, inviting tables and chairs, gorgeous potted plants, and perhaps a cat sunning itself. The interior of Hillbrook is just as inviting as the exterior. The house is filled with oriental rugs, warm, eclectic antiques, oil paintings and objects collected all over the world. The entire effect is very elegant.

Guests will stay in one of six guest rooms, all of which have private baths, delightful views, sitting areas, and air conditioning. The Bamford Suite is a large room with a welcoming fireplace, private porch, and queen size bed. A small bath has a square tub and shower combination. The Locke's Nest has its entrance high above the main living room, with both a double and a single brass bed. You'll enjoy a relaxing soak in the tub in the large sunny bath. A particularly memorable guest room, the Lookout has unusual angles and spaces created by the dramatically sloping walls of the house. It features an antique double bed and old fashioned claw foot tub. The Cottage is an intimate guest room accessible only from a private balcony overlooking the duck pond. The Cottage has a wood-burning stove, queen size bed, and tiled shower. The Point is an intriguing guest room tucked under the eaves of the kitchen. It has an antique double bed; the bath has a tub and shower. The Snuggery is another cozy guest room tucked under the eaves of the house. It can also be reached by an outside entrance, from a balcony overlooking the duck pond. This cozy dormered room has an antique double bed and a small jacuzzi tub.

The owner of Hillbrook Inn is Gretchen Carroll, who has operated Hillbrook for more than a decade. She lives on the grounds, but employs a full-time innkeeper. If you are interested in history, check out the spring house, where George Washington drank water on a visit to the property. The stream, Bull Skin Run, runs behind the house and across the grounds. However, it is not the history which draws individuals to Hillbrook Inn. It is its private sophistication, with great rooms and gourmet meals, for those not on a budget or a diet.

How to get there: From Charles Town, take Summit Point Road for approximately 5.5 miles. Make a left at the Bullskin Tavern sign.

Owner: Gretchen Carroll

Address/Telephone: Route 2, Box 152, Charles Town, WV 25414, 304-725-4223/800-304-4223, fax 304-725-4455.

Web page: www.hillbrookinn.com

Rooms: 6, all with private bath. Sorry, no young children or pets. No smoking in the dining areas.

Rates: $ 160. - 220. double occupancy weekdays; $ 240. - 300. double occupancy weekends. No reservations taken for one night stays except at the "procrastinator's rate" of $ 129. after 12:00 noon for that same evening. Rate includes a hearty country breakfast and afternoon tea. The seven-course dinner with wine is $ 70. per person. Payment may be by cash, check, Mastercard, Visa, or Discover. A 3% tax on the room, 6% sales tax, and 15% service fee will be added to the final bill. Call about special rates and packages.

Open: November - April, open Thursday through Sunday; May - October, open seven days a week.

Facilities and activities: Fax and library on premises. Gourmet meals, including seven course dinner; lovely grounds with patio, terraces, gardens, streams. Nearby are amenities of Charles Town, Martinsburg, Harpers Ferry and Berkeley Springs.

Washington House Inn

We pulled up in front of the Washington House Inn on an unseasonably hot day in June. Washington House looked like an oasis: big shade trees, lovely lawns and beds of impatiens, and a pretty front porch with comfortable wicker furniture. Inside this turn-of-the-century Victorian it was cool and comfortable, and our hostess Nina Vogel was warmly greeting guests. There are many good reasons to spend a weekend at the Washington House Inn, and foremost among them is your energetic and helpful hostess. Nina immediately makes you feel at home, serving cold beverages and helping guests find their way to the many attractions in the area. And did I mention that she is an excellent cook?

Nestled in the Blue Ridge Mountains, the Washington House Inn was built by descendants of George Washington's brothers, John Augustine and Samuel. The Vogels have operated it as a B & B since

1994. The carefully restored interiors are filled with lovely antique furnishings and beautiful woodwork.

There are six guest rooms at Washington House. Each is spacious and has a private bath, and such niceties as terry cloth robes and bottled water. There is an enchanting turret room, and rooms with antique and iron beds. Each guest room is decorated with attention to detail and has many Victorian touches.

Upon awakening at Washington House, come downstairs and help yourself to freshly brewed coffee or the gourmet selection of teas while you read *The Washington Post* on the front porch. When breakfast is served get ready for a real treat. Nina always has juice and seasonal fruits, served, if you like, with heavenly vanilla sauce or orange sour cream nut sauce. She also offers cereal and fresh baked goods. But don't fill up on the more traditional fare. Leave room for her egg sausage souffle, or caramelized apple French toast. As all the guests exclaimed over her breakfast, Nina obligingly passed out recipes to desirous guests. We found an interesting group of guests around the table. The large sunny dining room, the bountiful and delicious food, and the friendly conversation made breakfast at Washington House a memorable treat.

After breakfast take a stroll to charming Colonial Main Street, or the local museum and historical sites. To work off a little food, hike the mountain trails of the nearby Blue Ridge or bike along the C & O

Canal Towpath. Before you leave, say good-bye to Nina, who is one of the best innkeepers around.

How to get there: From Frederick, MD: take Route 340 and travel 24 miles, take a left on Route 9 East. Travel two blocks to 216 South George Street. From Leesburg, VA: take Route 7 West to Route 9 West. Travel 20 miles. Route 9 becomes South George Street.

Innkeepers: Mel and Nina Vogel

Address/Telephone: 216 South George Street, Charles Town, WV 25414, 304-725-7923/800-297-6957, fax 304-728-5150.

Web page: www.virtualcities.com/ons/wv/p/wvp3701.htm

E-mail: mnvogel@intrepid.net

Rooms: 6, all with private bath. Sorry, no pets or smoking. Children over ten years welcome.

Rates: $ 75 - 125. per night; includes full gourmet breakfast. Reservations recommended. Require one night's deposit. Accept Mastercard, Visa, American Express, Discover, Novus, personal check, cash.

Open: Year around.

Facilities and activities: Special events at the Inn include weddings, receptions, conference facilities, retreats. Nearby are antique shops, a history museum, community theater, Blue Ridge Mountains, Shenandoah and Potomac Rivers, Harpers Ferry, and Washington, D.C.

GERRARDSTOWN

Gerrardstown's Prospect Hill

A visit to Gerrardstown's Prospect Hill is like taking a deep breath of fresh air. Few sites can rival its peaceful backdrop of gentle hills and pastoral farmland. Located on a working farm, Prospect Hill is set among huge evergreens, and is approached by traveling over a quaint stone bridge. The stately house at Prospect Hill is of Federal design. You'll note the soaring chimney, and the brick laid in a distinctive Flemish bond pattern. Upon entering the spacious central hall, you'll immediately see the exquisite mural painted on the walls. The mural covers the walls from the front door, up the stairs, and goes all the way to the third floor. The mural has lovely green and yellow hills, and depicts scenes, people, and ships from colonial times.

Prospect Hill was built by William Wilson in 1794. Wilson's occupation was to outfit the wagon trains of the settlers heading west. The first family to live in the house, the Kelly family, were massacred by the Tucarora Indians. Enjoying the tranquility of the setting, it's hard to imagine such violence among these hills. There are several outbuildings on the property, including a six-hole outhouse. One small stone cottage, the former slave quarters, is available for rent. The cottage has a fireplace, private bath, and a small kitchen.

There are two spacious bedrooms for rent in the main house. They both have beautiful woodwork and cabinets, as well as private baths. The red guest room has both a double and a twin bed. Your hostess, Hazel Hudack, has furnished the house with original and family antiques. With its gentle patina of age, this handsome and elegant house remains extraordinarily comfortable.

The biggest draw for guests coming to Prospect Hill is the peace and quiet of its country setting. Prospect Hill's visitors enjoy walking the property, visiting with the farm animals, and observing the operations of growing hay and raising beef cattle. Fishermen will want to try their hand at the two fishing ponds on the property. I think I'd like to relax in the backyard, with some of Hazel's freshly baked cookies. Located just ten miles from Martinsburg, Prospect Hill is a delightful haven.

How to get there: From I-81 take Exit 5. Travel 3.25 miles west on Route 51 and Inn is on the left.

Innkeeper: Hazel Hudack

Address/Telephone: P.O. Box 135, Gerrardstown, WV 25420, 304-229-3346.

Rooms: 2 rooms in main house, each with private bath. Cottage also available, with fireplace, private bath and kitchen. Sorry, no smoking or pets. Children welcome in cottage.

Rates: $ 85. - 95; includes breakfast. Accept cash, personal check, and traveler's checks. Advance reservations required.

Open: Year around – unless snowed in.

Facilities and activities: Guests welcome to hike on the property, enjoy the farm animals and farm activities, as well as two fishing ponds. Nearby are Sleepy Creek Public Hunting and Fishing Grounds, historic Harpers Ferry, outlet malls in Martinsburg, and an antique mall in Bunker Hill.

Millcreek Manor Bed & Breakfast

The 100 year old Millcreek Manor Bed & Breakfast is located on 2.5 acres in historic Gerrardstown. Next door to the Manor is the historic Gerard House. Built in 1743, Gerard House is now home to a craft shop offering the wares of local artisans. The property where the Manor is located originally belonged to David Gerard, for whom Gerrardstown was named. Gerard was the first Baptist minister west of the Blue Ridge Mountains. Millcreek Manor was built in 1898 by Dr. Will Groff, a local dentist who installed the first gas and electrical lights in the area in his home.

Visitors to Millcreek Manor will enjoy its many outstanding architectural features. Late Victorian in style, the house has its original staircase, pine floors, and stained glass inserts in the dining and living room windows. All of the rooms in the house have traditional high ceilings, with the original baseboards, doors, and chair rails.

The porch, which runs across the front of the house, offers beautiful views of the Shenandoah Mountains. The formal dining room has lovely views of tree-filled lawns. The grounds are filled with many wonderful flowers, trees, and shrubs. The setting is very private, making it the perfect getaway.

There are two bedrooms for guests. The Victorian Room has a queen size bed, lovely cherry furniture, and Victorian touches. The second guest room has a full size brass bed, and is decorated in a country motif. The large shared bath has a tub, shower, and large vanity.

In addition to large country breakfasts, guests are also offered afternoon tea. Tea includes muffins and cookies, and coffee for coffee drinkers. Your hosts at Millcreek Manor will also prepare picnic baskets, upon request, for guests wishing to take lunch on a day trip. There is an additional charge for picnic lunches. Special diets can be accommodated with sufficient notice.

In addition to enjoying the grounds and porch at Millcreek, guests may choose to stroll through historic Gerrardstown, where many of the houses are 150 years old. Or, visit nearby Martinsburg, approximately ten miles away. There you'll find restaurants, antique shops, ghost walks, historic tours, Shenandoah National Park and outlet malls.

How to get there: From Route 81 take Exit 5 to Route 51 West. Go approximately 3 miles to a corner grocery in Gerrardstown. Turn left onto Virginia Line Road. Millcreek Manor is the third building on the left. It is a yellow house with a sign in front.

Innkeepers: Paul and Barbara Douglass

Address/Telephone: Box 78-0, Route 1, Gerrardstown, WV 25420, 304-229-1617.

Web page: www.travelwv.com/bed7.htm

Rooms: 2, with shared bath. Sorry, no smoking, pets, or children under 12.

Rates: $ 75. per night November to April; $ 85. from April to November. Includes hearty country breakfast. Accept cash, check, or money order.

Open: Year around except Christmas and New Year's Eve.

Facilities and Activities: 2.5 park-like acres and a front porch for relaxing; picnic table and television for guests' use. Nearby is historic Martinsburg with restaurants, antique shopping, as well as Shenandoah National Park.

GREAT CACAPON

Cross Flower Cottage & Animal Keep

Come stay for a week or a weekend at Cross Flower Cottage & Animal Keep. An 1800s hand-hewn log cabin built in Gettysburg, Pennsylvania, the cottage was moved to its present site in 1986. Cross Flower now has all the modern amenities, while remaining a cozy, rustic hideaway located at the edge of the woods.

There is no television or phone at the cottage, but most guests, many from the Washington area, seem to like it that way. Guests do have access to their hosts' telephone in emergencies. Visitors at Cross Flower usually enjoy sitting on the front porch swings, from where you can see your hosts' house, located across the pasture from the cottage. Guests are invited to visit the barn at feeding time, and pet the farm animals, cows, and very friendly dogs. Guests traveling with their own pet can have arrangements made for boarding. If your pet is a seasoned traveler, he can stay with you if he is kept on a leash when outside.

While staying at Cross Flower, you may want to visit nearby antique shops and mineral baths, take a trip on a scenic railroad, or enjoy the natural surroundings and the many animals. After enjoying yourself all day, at night you may want to dine in one of the fine area restaurants. Guests are also welcome to prepare meals in the cottage kitchen, which is equipped with a refrigerator and microwave. As you enjoy a cozy fire inside, you may get to watch deer eating right outside your window. Some visitors like a hot bath in the old fashioned claw foot tub, after which they enjoy a good night's sleep upstairs in the country sleigh bed. While the cottage is ideally suited for a couple, there is room upstairs in the loft for sleeping bags. There is also a small sofa downstairs which can serve as a child's bed.

Cross Flower is not air conditioned, but the fan in the cottage is usually plenty to keep everyone comfortable. Should the outside temperatures fall, get cozy in front of the toasty wood burning stove. The cottage is supplied with fresh towels and linens, and the cupboard is stocked with breakfast and snack foods, wine and sparkling cider. Your ambitious hosts, Laura Mechem and Sally Drury, have also added two additional cottages, called Olive Branch.

How to get there: From Maryland: take Route 522 South to Berkeley Springs. Go right at first stop light and continue on Route 9 West through Great Cacapon. From Maggio's General Store in Great Cacapon, go 5.6 miles on Route 9. Turn right on Mt. Nebo Road, go up the mountain and stay on the paved road. Pass pavilion and cemetery. At first farmhouse, bear left and go 1/3 mile. Look for Cross Flower sign. From Winchester, Virginia: Take Route 522 North to Berkeley Springs, make a left onto Route 9 and follow directions above.

Innkeepers: Laura Mechem and Sally Drury.

Address/Telephone: HC 62, Box 102 C, Great Cacapon, WV 25422, 304-947-7678, fax 304-947-5969.

Web page: http://wvweb.com/crossflowercottage/

E-mail: sdrury@intrepid.net

Rooms: One cottage available with private bath and kitchen. Children welcome. Pets can be boarded or stay with guests (if the pets are kept leashed and are well-trained seasoned travelers). Sorry, no smoking. Check out is noon.

Rates: $ 85. per night; $ 150. per weekend; special weekly rates available. Includes supplies for guests to make their own continental breakfast. A free week night (Monday through Thursday) is offered with any weekend. Accept Mastercard, Visa, American Express, personal check and cash.

Open: February through December.

Facilities and activities: On the premises are farm animals for petting, pasture and woodlands for short hikes, and games for playing at night in the cottage. Close to many historic towns and sites, including antique shops, mineral baths and massage, daily railroad trips, and beautiful natural scenery. Berkeley Springs, the C & O Canal, and the Paw Paw Tunnel are all only 15 minutes away. Shepherdstown and Harpers Ferry are 60 minutes away; Cumberland, MD is 40 minutes.

HARPERS FERRY

Angler's Inn

The Angler's Inn is a unique bed & breakfast located in a 110-year old house in historic Harpers Ferry. The Inn opened on July 4, 1997. The owners' friendly dogs, Buck, a golden retriever, and Jetta, a miniature greyhound, might greet you as you arrive. In addition to renting two charming guest rooms, your hosts, Debbi and Bryan Kelly, specialize in guided fishing trips that you may or may not coordinate with your visit. While Angler's Inn's specialty is fishing tours and lessons, visitors at the Inn do not have to fish, and participants of the fishing tours do not have to stay at the Inn. However, Angler's Inn does offer packages for those clients choosing to do both.

Clients going on the fishing trips can have any level of expertise. Each trip is limited to two persons, plus a guide. Clients choose whether they'd like to go in canoes or by jet boat. The main fishing guide and owner, Bryan Kelly, specializes in light line bass fishing; clients can also learn spin casting. The fishing trips are available as full day (eight hours) or half day (five hours) and include lunch, lures, and beverages.

There are two guest rooms for rent at the Inn. One bedroom has an adjacent suite, with a daybed and private bath. The other guest room has a sitting area and private bath. The Kelly's recently moved to Harpers Ferry from Baltimore, to pursue their dream of combining a bed & breakfast with Bryan's love for fishing. It's a great idea, offering options for a different kind of stay at a bed & breakfast.

How to get there: To reach Harpers Ferry from Maryland or Virginia, take Route 340 to town. Arriving in Harpers Ferry, travel to 846 Washington Street. The Inn is located next to the old Shipley School and across from the Women's Club. From Interstate 81, go west to Route 9, take Route 9 East to Charles Town. Next take Route 340 North to Harpers Ferry.

Innkeepers: Debbi and Bryan Kelly

Address/Telephone: 846 Washington Street, Harpers Ferry, WV 25425, 304-535-1239.

Web Page: www.theanglersinn.com

E-mail: info@theanglersinn.com

Rooms: 2, both with private bath. Children welcome over 12 years. Sorry, no smoking or pets.

Rates: $ 85. double occupancy; includes full sit down breakfast. Accept Mastercard, Visa, American Express, cash or personal check.

Open: Year around.

Facilities and activities: Specialize in guided fishing tours. Harpers Ferry is the site of historic battlefields, shopping, and antique shops. Nearby are the C & O Towpath for biking and hiking, and the Shenandoah and Potomac Rivers for fishing and canoeing. Also nearby are the baths at Berkeley Springs, horse and car racing in Charles Town, and outlet malls in Martinsburg.

Between the Rivers Bed & Breakfast

Enjoy a visit to the home of Elayne Edel and Wayne Bishop, and their friendly dog Nika, at Between the Rivers Bed & Breakfast. Located in the historic district of Harpers Ferry, the house was built in the 1890s, and has operated as a B & B for more than a decade. Guests will stay in The Cottage, which has a queen size bed and a private bath with an oversized whirlpool tub. All guests receive a full breakfast in their private quarters. There is a small outdoor play area for children, and a rabbit for them to visit with, as well.

In addition to spending time relaxing in their room, guests can get involved with the history of the region. Within walking distance is Harpers Ferry National Park. For real Civil War buffs, the Antietam and Gettysburg Battlefields are easily accessible.

Shoppers will enjoy local stores featuring antiques and collectibles. The historic C & O Canal Towpath, which runs from Harpers Ferry to Georgetown in Washington, is great for walking, hiking, biking, and cross-country skiing. The nearby Appalachian Trail, which extends from Georgia to Maine, is a special favorite for hikers. For fishing, rafting, canoeing and wading, try the beautiful Shenandoah and Potomac Rivers.

How to get there: From Virginia or Maryland: take Route 340 over the Shenandoah River Bridge in West Virginia. Turn at stop light to Bolivar, go through Bolivar on Washington Street into Harpers Ferry. From Washington Street in Harpers Ferry, turn onto Gilmore Street. The B & B is on the corner of Gilmore and Ridge Streets.

Innkeepers: Elayne Edel and Wayne Bishop

Address/Telephone: 500 E. Ridge Street, Harpers Ferry, WV 25425, 304-535-2768

Rooms: One cottage with queen size bed and private bath. Full breakfast is served in your quarters. Children welcome and port-a-cribs available. Sorry, no pets or smoking.

Rates: $ 85. weekdays; $ 95. weekends and holidays. Cash or personal check welcome.

Open: All year.

Facilities and activities: Harpers Ferry National Park; the Appalachian Trail and the C & O Canal Towpath for walking, hiking, biking or cross-country skiing. The Shenandoah and Potomac Rivers offer fishing, rafting, canoeing and wading.

Briscoe House

Make plans to stay at Briscoe House, a bed and breakfast located in a 110-year old house in historic Harpers Ferry. Your charming hosts Jean and Lin Hale, originally from England, look forward to making your stay as enjoyable as possible. In the morning they will serve you a full English breakfast, giving you the energy to take in all the sites and activities in Harpers Ferry and the Panhandle.

There are two large suites available for guests at Briscoe House. Appropriately, they are the English Ivy Suite and the English Rose Suite. The English Rose is decorated in pink and white, with roses everywhere to sweeten your dreams. This suite has a large white iron bed, a sitting area with a sleep sofa, and a private bath. The bath has a large jacuzzi tub and even an English Rose shower curtain. The English Ivy Suite is decorated in green and white, with an ivy motif winding throughout. This suite has also has a sitting area, as well as an enormous private bath, complete with a huge jacuzzi tub.

On the upstairs landing there is a "self-serve" coffee and tea bar, with the fixings for guests to help themselves when the mood strikes. After you have relaxed at Briscoe House, your hosts can give you information on nearby historic and recreational activities. Harpers Ferry is a good location from which to tour Civil War sites, bike the C & O Canal Towpath, or day hike on the Appalachian Trail. You can also raft, canoe, or kayak on the Shenandoah and Potomac Rivers. At the very least guests should walk to the point in town where one can see the two rivers converge.

How to get there: From Virginia or Maryland: take Route 340 over the Shenandoah River Bridge in West Virginia. Turn at stop light to Bolivar, go through Bolivar on Washington Street into Harpers Ferry. Briscoe House is located at 828 Washington Street.

Innkeepers: Jean and Lin Hale

Address/Telephone: 828 Washington Street, Harpers Ferry, WV 25425, 304-535-2416.

Rooms: 2 large suites, both with private bath. Sorry, no pets or smoking. Call about children.

Rates: $ 75. weekdays, $ 85. weekends, and $ 95. holidays. Includes full English breakfast. Accept Mastercard, Visa, American Express, and Discover.

Open: All year.

Facilities and activities: Nearby attractions include Charles Town Race Track, Antietam Battlefield, Virginia wineries, Summit Point Auto Racing, Blue Ridge Outlet Center, and C & O Towpath.

Harpers Ferry Guest House Bed & Breakfast

Enjoy West Virginia's "almost heavenly" hospitality at the Harpers Ferry Guest House Bed & Breakfast. Your hosts, Al and Allison Alsdorf, are very pleasant and will make you feel comfortable right away. The house itself is of new construction, but was designed to look like an old Victorian. The exterior of the house was designed by a family friend, Kip, who is also the mayor of Harpers Ferry. Al Alsdorf designed the inside of the house, and also runs a frame shop in the basement of the house. The house has central air conditioning, and private off-street parking.

The house is cozy, as well as being handicapped accessible, and is filled with comfortable antiques, reproductions, charming braided rugs and quilts. There are two guest rooms for rent, each one spacious and having a private bath. The two rooms each have lovely four-poster beds, which were hand made in West Virginia. A night's stay includes a full breakfast, featuring a combination of fruit, muffins, waffles, French toast, or omelets.

You'll not lack for anything to do while staying here, as the list of points of interest in the area is extensive: the Appalachian Trail, Antietam Battlefield, the Brunswick Railroad Museum, C & O Canal and Museum, Charles Town Opera House, Shepherdstown Opera House, Harpers Ferry National Park, and the Summit Point Road Races. Your hosts are more than happy to answer questions and help you find out about local activities.

For shoppers, galleries, shops, antiquing and country auctions all will lure you to part with some money. Also within walking distance are many fine restaurants. For guests who are outdoors enthusiasts, you can enjoy canoeing, golfing, tubing, rafting, biking, hiking, and fishing. Whew! I'm worn out thinking about all the possibilities.

How to get there: From Virginia or Maryland: take Route 340 over the Shenandoah River Bridge in West Virginia. The Guest House is off Route 340. Turn at stop light to Bolivar, go through Bolivar on Washington Street in Harpers Ferry, go one block past the post office. Turn left off Jackson Street; the house is on the corner of Washington and Jackson Streets, at 800 Washington Street.

Innkeepers: Al and Allison Alsdorf

Address/Telephone: 800 Washington Street, Harpers Ferry, WV 25425, 304-535-6955.

Web page: www.intrepid.net/guesthouse

E-mail: alsdorf@harpersferrywv.com

Rooms: 2, each with a queen size bed and a private bath. Please, no smoking or children under 10. Check out at 11:00 a.m.

Rates: $ 65. weekdays; $ 91. Friday or Saturday. Includes full breakfast. Cash or personal check welcome.

Open: All year.

Facilities and activities: Numerous historical points of interest, including Harpers Ferry National Historical Park and the C & O Canal and Museum. Many sporting activities available, including hiking, biking, canoeing and golfing.

Hilltop House Hotel

Perched on a spectacular site high above the confluence of the Potomac and Shenandoah Rivers, Hilltop House Hotel and Conference Center is a Harpers Ferry institution. Few visit Harpers Ferry without stopping at Hilltop House to enjoy its majestic view, from where one can see the foothills and ridges of Virginia, West Virginia, and Maryland. When Thomas Jefferson visited Harpers Ferry, he remarked on the very view you'll have from many of Hilltop's rooms, calling "the meeting of the Potomac and Shenandoah Rivers and the encircling mountains 'worth a voyage across the Atlantic'." If you make a trip through the parking lot at Hilltop House, you will see license plates from all over the Mid-Atlantic region, as well as cars covered with rafting gear, canoes, and mountain bikes. Hilltop House is considered the perfect place to stay by many outdoor enthusiasts.

Since its beginning in 1888, Historic Hilltop House has offered visitors beautiful vistas, a warm bed, and a gracious meal. Such prominent persons as Alexander Graham Bell, Mark Twain, Pearl Buck, and President Woodrow Wilson have enjoyed stays at the hotel. Hilltop House has managed to maintain its relaxed but gracious ambiance for over 100 years.

Hilltop House has 64 guest rooms for rent. The hotel offers a wide variety of rooms and suites with different bed sizes and amenities. The restaurant at Hilltop House is open for breakfast, lunch, and dinner. On Friday, Saturday, and Sunday they offer their famous buffet; guests can enjoy afternoon tea on Wednesdays at 3 p.m. Hilltop House is located just a short walk from downtown historic Harpers Ferry, with its shops, Civil War history, and picturesque streets.

How to get there: From WV Route 340, take Washington Street into Harpers Ferry. The hotel is located at the end of Ridge Street, which lies parallel to Washington and is one block to the left as you enter town.

Innkeeper: Mr. William H. Stanhagen

Address/Telephone: 400 East Ridge Street, Harpers Ferry, WV, 25425, 304-535-2132/800-338-8319, fax 304-535-6322.

Web page: http://wvweb.com/www/HHH

E-mail: wstanhagen@aol.com

Rooms: 64 rooms, all with private bath. Wide variety of suites and options. Children welcome; sorry, no pets. Smoking permitted in some areas.

Rates: $ 65. - 150. per night. Full restaurant open for breakfast, lunch, and dinner. Accept all major credit cards. AARP discount of 10%; conference discounts available.

Open: Year around.

Facilities and activities: Offer full restaurant, facilities for conferences and special events, beautiful views, some rooms have jacuzzi tubs. Nearby are white water rafting, tubing, Civil War sites, Appalachian Trail headquarters, and the C & O Towpath for hiking and biking.

Ranson-Armory House B & B

The handsome Ranson-Armory House is Federal in style, with Victorian influences seen in rounded corners, archways, and the dining room windows. Several additions to the house were made around the turn-of-the-century. The original house was built by the Federal government in 1837-38 as quarters for the management personnel of the United States Armory. In 1859 the house was occupied by John E..P. Daingerfield, the armory paymaster.

After the Civil War, Dr. Briscoe B. Ranson, of the 12th Virginia Cavalry, bought the house around 1880. In 1903 Dr. Ranson added a wing to the rear of the house, doubling its size. In 1905, Dr. Ranson added "a fine operating room" to the rear of the house. Patients entered through a side door which is now closed. Ranson family members occupied the house for 60 years. The house is now a popular bed & breakfast operated by John and Dorothy Hughes. Your hosts are very knowledgeable about the entire eastern panhandle, and will be happy to help you with your plans.

There are two guest bedrooms from which to choose. Each of these have a double bed and private bath. Guests are invited to enjoy the living room, as well as several porches, the patio, and garden in season. During the period of peak fall foliage – September and October – a three week advance reservation is recommended. A full country breakfast accompanies your visit, and guests are allowed to bring their own beverages during their stay.

The Ranson-Armory House is within walking distance to the "Lower Town" of Harpers Ferry, where evening dining is available. The Appalachian Trail and C & O Towpath are easily accessible for hiking and biking, and many other sporting activities are available in the area. The closest large town is Charles Town, population 5,000, eight miles away.

How to get there: To reach Harpers Ferry from Maryland or Virginia, take Route 340 to town. The B & B is one mile off Route 340 at 690 Washington Street. From I-81, go west to Route 9; take Route 9 East to Charles Town and 340 North to Harpers Ferry.

Innkeepers: John and Dorothy Hughes

Address/Telephone: 690 Washington Street, Harpers Ferry, WV 25425, 304-535-2142.

Rooms: Two, both with double bed and private bath. Twin bed or rollaway available. Sorry, no children under 10, pets, or smoking.

Rates: $ 65. weekdays; $ 75. - 80. weekends, double occupancy. Includes full breakfast. Mastercard, Visa, American Express, cash and personal check with identification are all welcome. Deposit required by credit card or mail.

Open: All year.

Facilities and activities: Available nearby: white water rafting, hiking, biking; also the Antietam Battlefield and Jefferson County Courthouse, the site of the John Brown trial.

HEDGESVILLE

O'Brien's Cabins

The O'Brien's rent two secluded cabins and one cottage on eighty wooded acres. Their business and property is a nature preserve. The focus is your enjoyment, and the preservation of, Mother Nature. Your privacy, peace, and quiet are thereby guaranteed. Each building sits in a secluded setting surrounded by trees, with nature trails available for exploring the property. You'll find a one acre pond for tubing and swimming on the property, and the Potomac river is just 1.5 miles away.

The cabins have a kitchen and living area, bedroom with double bed, loft with double bed, full bath, and a deck. On chilly nights, there is a cozy, warm wood stove in addition to electric heat. Towels and linens are provided. In warm weather, soak in an antique claw foot bathtub on the deck or in the bedroom of the cottage.

The O'Briens offer free ecology tours to all guests. Their motto: Solitude is not a privilege – it's a right and necessity.

How to get there: From I-81, take Exit 16 west to Cherry Run Road in Morgan County. On Cherry Run Road, go 1.5 miles to a driveway marked with a mailbox reading O'Brien.

Innkeepers: David and Kristine O'Brien

Address/Telephone: Route 3, Box 401 H, Hedgesville, WV 25427, 304-754-9128.

Web page: www.berkeleysprings.com/obriens2/

Rooms: Each cabin is 520 square feet with 2 double beds, a full bath, and a basic kitchen. The cottage is 800 square feet and sleeps 4 persons. Coffee, tea, and granola are supplied in each unit. Children welcome; sorry, no pets or smoking.

Rates: $ 115. per couple on weekdays; $ 125. for two per day on weekends (2 day minimum); $ 525. for two adults weekly. Cottage rates are based upon number of persons. Cash or personal check accepted.

Open: All year.

Facilities and activities: A 20 minute drive to Berkeley Springs offers massages, mineral baths, antique shopping and great restaurants.

The cabins are located near Sleepy Creek, a 20,000 acre wildlife preserve with hiking and a 200 acre lake for boating and fishing. The historic C & O Canal, Paw Paw Tunnel, and Prospect Peak are all nearby. Canoe and bike rental, golf and skiing are also available nearby.

The Farmhouse at Tomahawk Run

The Farmhouse at Tomahawk Run is nestled in a valley along a stream called Tomahawk Run. Surrounding the Farmhouse are 280 acres of woods, hills, and meadows, with walking paths and gardens maintained for guests' enjoyment. The land was originally settled in the early 1740s by Israel Robinson and his wife, who hailed from Northern Ireland. They ended their search for a new home site when they found a clear spring, flowing into a rock basin shaped like a tomahawk. The spring soon became known as Tomahawk Spring, and Robinson received a land grant of 400 acres from Lord Fairfax. The current owners, Judy and Hugh Erskine, are descendants of the Robinson's, the original settlers. The property has never left the family.

The Farmhouse was built during the Civil War. It underwent extensive restoration and expansion in 1991. As many of the original materials as possible were used during the restoration. The Farmhouse has 3 guest rooms, all with private baths. Two guest rooms have king size beds, sitting areas, and private balconies. The third room has a queen size pencil post bed, with a private adjoining sitting room. Your hosts will prepare a delicious three course breakfast for you in the morning. During cold weather, guests often enjoy a roaring fire in the large stone fireplace. Warmer days often find visitors enjoying the view from the rocking chairs, or from the jacuzzi, on the large wraparound porch.

In addition to the Farmhouse, the Erskines also have a Carriage House on the property which is rented to guests. The Carriage House has two bedrooms and two bathrooms on the upper level. Downstairs is a complete kitchen/living/dining area. One guest room has a king size bed; the other has both a queen and a single. Both bedrooms open onto a large covered balcony. The living area has a fireplace, sofa bed, television, and VCR. The Erskines have provided all the amenities needed to make your stay comfortable, as well as a setting to ensure a tranquil stay.

How to get there: From I-81,take WV Exit 16 West. Follow Route 9 for 6 miles (2 miles past Hedgesville traffic light) to Route 7 (Tomahawk Road). Turn left, go 2.5 miles, take a sharp right soon after Tomahawk Christian Church and just before the Tomahawk Valley Store. Go .5 mile to The Farmhouse at Tomahawk Run, which is on the left.

Innkeepers: Judy and Hugh Erskine

Address/Telephone: 1 Tomahawk Run Place, Hedgesville, WV 25427, 304-754-7350, fax 304-754-7350.

Web page: www.travelwv.com/bed5.htm

E-mail: tomahawk@intrepid.net

Rooms: 3 in Farmhouse, all with private bath. 2 in Carriage House, both with private bath. Sorry, no pets or smoking. Small children are welcome in the Carriage House. Check out time is 11 a.m.

Rates: $ 85. for the Farmhouse; $ 150. for the Carriage House for four persons. includes a full three-course breakfast and afternoon tea. Group and extended stay rates are available. Accept Mastercard, Visa, Discover, cash, or personal check.

Open: All year, except closed mid-January through mid-February.

Facilities and activities: On premises: 1.5 miles of walking paths through 280 acres overlooking valley and hills. Brook with viewing benches on property. Cross country skiing available in winter. Nearby are many Civil War areas of interest: Charles Town, Martinsburg, Harpers Ferry, and Antietam. Also nearby are horseback riding, golf, Berkeley Springs State Park, and Cacapon State Park.

MARTINSBURG

Boydville, The Inn at Martinsburg

For a retreat from the modern day rush, treat yourself to a stay at Boydville, the Inn at Martinsburg. Traveling down the lovely lane of maples, which lead to the impressive boxwood circle and the stately house, you'll know you've reached a special destination. Visited by General Stonewall Jackson during the Civil War, the land was once part of a large plantation purchased by General Elisha Boyd in the 1790s. Boydville now consists of the Inn and several outbuildings on ten lovely acres of stately trees and boxwoods.

All six bedrooms are furnished with functional American and English antiques. Downstairs, with private baths, are the Adam Stephen Room, with a double bed; and the Stonewall Jackson Room, with a queen size bed. Upstairs, with private baths, are the Elisha Boyd Room, with a double bed and a single; and the Charles Faulkner Room, with a queen size bed. The two rooms upstairs – which share a bath — are the Mary Boyd Room and the Belle Boyd Room, each having a twin bed. Included with your room is an "expanded Continental" breakfast, including one home-baked item, coffee cake, cereal, fruit, juice, coffee, tea, and milk. Native West Virginia products are featured in season.

Guests at Boydville enjoy more than just their room at the Inn. The house is full of fine craftsmanship from an earlier time, including fine woodwork, window glass, and the foyer wallpaper, hand painted in England especially for Boydville. A hand painted French mural from the 1830s graces a bedroom wall. French chandeliers in the Inn were brought to Boydville by General Boyd's son-in-law, Charles Faulkner. Faulkner was ambassador to France before and during the Civil War.

Guests usually enjoy exploring the ten acres surrounding the Inn, including the ivy-covered brick walled courtyard and gardens. Double parlors are perfect for conversation or reading. Admiring the 100 year old boxwood from the porch rockers is always a popular pastime at Boydville.

In addition to serving individual travelers, Boydville is a unique retreat for business meetings, and a romantic setting for special events, including weddings. The Inn can accommodate up to 20 persons for meetings and dinners, and up to 150 persons for receptions.

How to get there: From I-81 take Exit 13 (King Street). Go east on

King Street to the town center, go right on Queen Street at the library. Go three blocks and look for a historic marker on the right marking the Inn. Turn into the long drive on the right.

Innkeeper: LaRue Frye

Address/Telephone: 601 South Queen Street, Martinsburg, WV 25401, 304-263-1448.

Rooms: 6, 4 with private bath, 2 with shared bath. Full breakfast. Sorry, no smoking or pets. Children 12 and over are welcome. Check out is 11:00 a.m.

Rates. $ 100. - 125. per night. 10% discount for 3 nights stay or longer. Accept Mastercard, Visa, personal check or cash.

Open: All year, except August and December 20 - January 1.

Facilities and activities: Ten acres of grounds with a courtyard and garden, wraparound porch with rockers. Can host business meetings and weddings. Two national parks and many historical sites are nearby. Also nearby are white water rafting, auctions, crafts, golf, Berkley Springs mineral baths, shopping on Main Street in Martinsburg and historic Harper's Ferry.

The Pulpit and Palette Inn

The Pulpit and Palette Inn is located in a home whose history dates prior to the Civil War. In 1839, Alexander Stephen sold the land to Jacob Gardner. Alexander Stephen was the brother of Adam Stephen, the founder of Martinsburg. In early 1870, Gardner's son, John Smith Gardner, built the main structure – a three-story wood frame Victorian house.

As guests approach the bed and breakfast in this century, they notice its bright Victorian paint colors, handsome wrought iron fence, and lovely flower gardens, tended to by your hosts, Bill and Janet Starr. Your hosts' occupations gave the Inn its name, and you will see Janet Starr's artwork throughout the house. (Guess what Bill's occupation is?) The Inn has two guest rooms for rent, which share a bath. Guests are invited to enjoy afternoon tea, as well as evening hors d'oeuvres and drinks, in the interesting front parlor. The Starrs have spent many years abroad, and precious objects from their interesting travels can be seen throughout the house. Your stay at the Pulpit and Palette Inn includes a full breakfast.

How to get there: From Route 81 take Exit 13, for "King Street Downtown." Follow King Street into Martinsburg. Travel to the third traffic light and go right onto Winchester Avenue. Travel one block and turn left on John's Street. The Inn is the second house on the left, visible by its bright magenta trim.

Innkeepers: Bill and Janet Starr

Address/Telephone: 516 West John Street, Martinsburg, WV 25401, 304-263-7012.

Web page: www.travelwv.com/bed1.htm

E-mail: bstarr28@earthlink.net

Rooms: 2, with shared bath. Sorry, no children under 12, pets, or smoking.

Rates: $ 65. single occupancy; $ 80. double. Full breakfast included. Accept Visa, Mastercard, personal check or cash. Discounts for extended stays.

Open: Year around, except closed in January.

Facilities and activities: Nearby are historic Harpers Ferry, Antietam Battlefield, Skyline Drive, Bunker Hill Antique Mall, Boarman House Center for the Arts, and antique and craft shops.

PAW PAW

Paw Paw Patch

The Paw Paw Patch is the only lodging located in Paw Paw, a small town located on the C & O Towpath. This B & B, located within 1 mile of the path, actually offers the only lodging in the town. The National Park Service includes the Paw Paw Patch in their informational materials, resulting in most of the Paw Paw's guests being bicyclists from the trail.

Of course, some travelers along the trail just stumble upon the place, as happened to the Paw Paw's first, and most famous, guest. One weekend, the owners of the house were out of town, and their daughter and her friend were staying at the house alone. A gentleman came to the door, asking where in town he could find a night's lodging. Looking at each other, the girls told the gentleman that there was no place to stay in town. After a brief discussion, it was determined that the man would rent a room for the night. One of the girls kept staring at the man, and giggling. When asking what was so funny, the non-giggling girl told the man that her friend thought he looked like Art Garfunkel. . . . After a quick smile, the man told them that he was Art Garfunkel. Upon their return, the girl's parents heard the story, and decided to open their home as a bed & breakfast.

You'll find the Paw Paw Patch located near the trail between Cumberland and Hancock, about 30 miles from either, with no other place to stay in between. The Paw Paw has three bedrooms for rent. One has a double bed, one has two twin beds, and one has both a double and a twin bed. The rooms are modest and attractive, with cozy quilts on the beds. Two of the rooms have air conditioning, and the other has a fan. Your hosts are very friendly and warm, and make visitors feel at home. A full breakfast is served with a night's stay.

How to get there: From Cumberland, take Route 51 East to Paw Paw. From Winchester take 522 North to Route 127, to Route 29 to Route 9. From Berkeley Springs take Route 9 West to Paw Paw. Paw Paw is at the intersection of Route 51 and 29, at 402 Winchester Street.

Innkeepers: Bill and Kay Miller

Address/Telephone: P. O. Box 291, Paw Paw, WV 25434, 304-947-7496.

Rooms: 3, all with shared bath. Sorry, no smoking or pets. Children welcome with responsible parents.

Rates: $ 45. single occupancy; $ 55. double. Includes full breakfast. Accept cash or personal check.

Open: All year.

Facilities and activities: C & O Canal Tow Path for bicyclists; also nearby are the Potomac and Cacapon Rivers.

ROMNEY

Hampshire House 1884

The Simmons' would like to invite you to come for a visit at Hampshire House 1884. Enjoy the charm of the 1880s in this completely restored period inn . . . with the modern amenities of air conditioning, private baths, television, and sound proofing. Hampshire House is located in a small sleepy hamlet named Romney, which some consider the oldest town in West Virginia. Romney lies on the beautiful South Branch of the Potomac River.

Guests can choose from five different guest rooms. The Lamplighter Room is located on the first floor. It offers an attached bath with an alcohol burning fireplace. Its rosewood bedroom suite is circa 1860, and has a queen size bed. The Whitacre Room is named after the second owners of the house. It has an attached bath, an alcohol burning fireplace, and is furnished with an Eastlake style bedroom suite, circa 1882. The bed is a full size. The Russell Room also has an alcohol burning fireplace. It is furnished with a circa 1840 full size cannon ball bed, accessed by a step stool. A private bath is just down the hall. This room is named after the Russell family, who completed construction of the house in 1884. The Rebecca Room can adjoin the Russell Room if desired. Originally the children's room, the Rebecca Room now has a cast iron queen size bed and attached bath. Jane chose the name because Rebecca was a popular name in the late 1800s, and means "one who gives food and drink to the stranger." The Monroe Room is named after Miss Ethel Monroe. She, the third owner, occupied the house from 1901 to 1927. This room has an attached bath with an 1890s full size brass bed and an 1840s Jenny Lind single bed.

Guests are encouraged to spend time in the Music Room, with its 1887 pump organ. This room is also stocked with books, video tapes, a VCR, magazines, games, and a gas fireplace. The Parlor has an electric fireplace and provides a more intimate place for visiting. Visitors to Hampshire House also enjoy relaxing on the cozy patio in the private back yard. The garden-patio is named after the fourth owner of the house, Mrs. Minnie Peters, an avid gardener. Hampshire House is noted for its full country breakfasts and the special attention paid to its guests.

How to get there: From I-68 East take Exit 43A in Cumberland, MD. Follow signs to WV Route 28 South via Ridgeley, WV. From 28 South, turn left on Rosemary Lane, then turn left one block on Grafton

Street. From Southern D.C, take I-66 West to VA Route 17 North to Route 50 West through Winchester. Take Route 50 West to Romney. Turn right on Grafton Street at the Bank of Romney.

Innkeepers: Jane and Scott Simmons

Address/Telephone: 165 North Grafton Street, Romney, WV 26757, 304-822-7171.

Web page: http://wvweb.com/www/hampshire_chamber/HampshireHouse.htm/

Rooms: 5, all private baths. Sorry, no pets or smoking. Please call about children.

Rates. $ 65. - 90. per night, double occupancy. Includes full breakfast. Accept American Express, Visa, Mastercard, Discover, Diners Club or personal check.

Open: Year around.

Facilities and activities: In the area: antique shopping, canoeing, fishing, the C & O Canal Towpath, Civil War Earth Works, golfing, hiking, massage, and winery tours.

SHEPHERDSTOWN

Bavarian Inn and Lodge

The Bavarian Inn was built in 1930 as a private residence. The stately "Greystone Mansion," as it was called, sits on eleven lovely acres and was converted into an inn in 1962. Since that time it has hosted many guests, including prominent politicians and dignitaries. Extensive renovations were done to the Inn in 1977 and 1984. The Inn is owned by native Bavarian, Erwin Asam, and his wife Carol. One major draw of the Inn is its award winning restaurant. Its elegant dining rooms are filled with antiques and deer horn chandeliers. The menu is international in flavor, with German and American specialties. At any time the menu may include such offerings as roast pheasant and wild boar.

The Bavarian Inn has 72 elegantly furnished rooms, all with private baths, color television and fireplaces. Many of the rooms also have four-poster beds, fireplaces, and sitting areas. For special weekends there are deluxe suites with fireplaces and whirlpool bathtubs. In addition to lovely rooms, guests often enjoy relaxing pool side or on the sun deck. Others enjoy a workout in the exercise room or taking in the view of the Potomac.

The Inn's clients include friends and relatives of students at Shepherd College; others are politicians from the Washington area. While in Shepherdstown, enjoy the antique shops, boutiques, restaurants, and cultural activities, many at the College. Nearby are historic Harpers Ferry, the Charles Town Racetrack, outlet shopping in Martinsburg, and the nation's oldest health spa in Berkeley Springs.

How to get there: From Washington: Take I-270 to Frederic Bypass, then I-70 to Exit 49; turn left on 40 Alt. to Braddock Hts.-Boonsboro. Turn left in Boonsboro on MD 34 to Shepherdstown. From Leesburg, VA: Take Route 9 through Charles Town to Kearneysville, turn right on Route 480 to Shepherdstown.

Innkeepers: Erwin and Carol Asam

Address/Telephone: Route 1, Box 30, Shepherdstown, WV 25443, 304-876-2551.

Web page: http://wvweb.com/www/bavarian_inn

Rooms: 72, all with private bath. Sorry, no pets. Children welcome. Smoking and non-smoking rooms are available. Check out is 12 noon.

Rates: $ 65. - 165.; Royal Suite is $ 195. - 275. Rates vary due to day of the week, holidays, and the peak fall foliage season. Restaurant serves breakfast, lunch, and dinner. Accepts major credit cards.

Open: Year around.

Facilities and activities: Large conference facilities, award winning restaurant, color television, telephone. Many rooms have a fireplace and sitting area. Special suites available with whirlpool baths. All guests can enjoy outdoor pool, exercise rooms, sun deck, tennis courts and bike rental. Nearby are golf, white water rafting, canoeing, and the C & O Canal Towpath.

The Thomas Shepherd Inn

The stately Thomas Shepherd Inn was built around 1850, originally as a Lutheran parsonage on land once owned by Thomas Shepherd. Early in this century it served as the office and home of several prominent physicians, and in 1984 it was painstakingly restored and re-furnished to its original period ambiance. A visit to the Thomas Shepherd Inn will be filled with the graciousness of the hospitable past, the glow of a friendly fireside, and the delicious gourmet food of your host, Margaret Perry.

The Inn has seven lovely guest rooms, all with private baths and air conditioning. There are also a living room, two formal dining rooms, library and porch to be shared and enjoyed by visitors. In addition to the gourmet breakfast that is included with your lodging, guests can request specially prepared dinners and picnic lunches for an additional fee, and with sufficient notice.

Margaret can describe many of the delights of Shepherdstown, a small but cosmopolitan community which is generally recognized as West Virginia's oldest. Hunt for authentic antiques, intriguing arts and crafts, and the finest furnishings for the home on German Street. Take in the offerings of the historic Shepherdstown Museum, the Millbrook Orchestra, and Shepherd College's Contemporary American Theater Festival. When you've covered the town, return to the Inn, sip sherry in front of the fire, and envision yourself a guest in an elegant mid-nineteenth century home.

How to get there: From I-81 to Martinsburg, take the Shepherd College exit. Take Route 45 to Shepherdstown. Inn is at corner of German and Duke Streets.

Innkeeper: Margaret Perry

Address/Telephone: 300 West German Street, P. O. Box 1162, Shepherdstown, WV 25443, 304-876-3715/888-889-8952, fax 304-876-3313.

Web page: www.intrepid.net/thomas_shepherd

E-mail: mrg@intrepid.net

Rooms: 7, all with private bath. Sorry, no pets or smoking. Children welcome at eight years of age.

Rates: Sundays through Thursdays, $ 85. - 95. Fridays, Saturdays, and holidays, $ 95. - 135. Includes full gourmet breakfast. Picnic lunch with 24 hours notice. Accept Visa, Mastercard and American Express.

Open: All year.

Facilities and activities: Many outdoor activities in the area, including golf, river rafting, biking on the C & O Towpath, and hiking on the Appalachian Trail. Other spots of interest include the Contemporary American Theater Festival, Antietam Battlefield, Rumsey Monument, Thomas Shepherd Grist Mill and the Berkeley Springs Mineral Baths.

MONONGOHELA FOREST REGION

Durbin, Elkins, Helvetia, Hillsboro, Huntersville, Huttonsville, Marlinton, Moorefield, Montrose, Slatyfork, Valley Head

About the region . . .

Elkins, home to Davis & Elkins College, was recently selected as one of the top 50 American small towns in which to live. It was also named as one of the "top 50 small art towns." One big reason for the award of the latter is the presence of the Augusta Heritage Center for the Traditional Folk Arts, which offers concerts and workshops throughout the year. Perhaps best known is the "Augusta Heritage Festival" (a several week-long celebration of traditional music and arts) held each summer at Davis & Elkins College. Although Elkins is home to many excellent bed & breakfasts, you'll still need to book your rooms early during the Festival.

As important to Elkins as the arts, or arguably more, are the outdoor activities available in the region, many in the 840,000 acre Monongahela State Forest. The Elkins area has a national reputation for its spectacular mountain biking. The nearby town of Davis is home to the "24 Hours of Canaan" Mountain Bike Race. A less well-known asset is the region's excellent fly fishing, but this secret is spreading. Many mountain biking enthusiasts and fly fishermen are flocking to the small community of **Slatyfork**. There you will find The Inn at Elk River, which hosts bike workshops throughout the year, as well as fly fishing excursions. Of course, skiing has always been popular in the area – the region boasts three major ski resorts. Down the road from Slatyfork is the charming town of **Huttonsville**, which has many lovely bed and breakfasts for weary sportsmen or seasoned travelers.

After enjoying the glorious Monongahela State Forest, you may want to visit the charming community of **Helvetia**. Swiss immigrants settled Helvetia and several surrounding communities in the 1800s. Evidence of their heritage is everywhere. Home and barn construction, food, music, and other customs still bear the marks of the early Swiss, giving the area a special charm and unique character. Helvetians love to celebrate, especially at their unique annual festivals. The most traditionally Swiss of the celebrations is *Fasnacht*, a ritual chasing away Old Man Winter. Visitors are invited to join townspeople in donning costumes for a masked ball, after which an effigy of Old Man Winter is burned on a bonfire. *Fascnacht* takes place on the Saturday before Ash Wednesday. The local ramp dinner is held at the end of April each year; the Helvetia Fair is held annually on the second weekend in September.

Among the many quaint towns in this region is **Marlinton**. Located on the Greenbrier River Trail, this small town is a mecca for outdoor enthusiasts wanting to enjoy the lure of the trail and the river. You can canoe, kayak, or float along the river; the trail is great for hiking, biking, and horseback riding. The Current is the only B & B actually located directly on the Greenbrier River Trail.

DURBIN

Cheat Mountain Club

Cheat Mountain Club was built in 1887 by the Cheat Mountain Sportsmen's Association. From that day on, the Club has been a special, gracious retreat where visitors can enjoy comfortable lodging, good food, and pleasant company while they take advantage of the recreational opportunities of this spectacular setting. The Club is situated along the Shavers Fork River, a source of great trout fishing, and is surrounded by the 840,000 acre Monongahela National Forest. The historic guest register of the Club records the visit of Thomas Edison, Henry Ford, and Harvey Firestone, who stayed here in 1918.

There are ten guest rooms at Cheat Mountain Club. One is a suite with a king size bed and private bath. Nine of the guest rooms have a wash basin and medicine chest in the room, with men and women's full baths available nearby. Guests will receive special attention from the Club's chef, who prepares three family-style meals every day. His specialties include country breakfasts, hearty stews, and home-made pastries. Special requests can be accommodated with sufficient notice.

Outdoor opportunities while staying at Cheat Mountain Club are almost endless. In the summer, Shavers Fork River is ideal for canoeing, kayaking and rafting. Guests can explore the private hiking and biking trails of the Club's 180 acres, or explore the nearby Allegheny and Greenbrier River trails. Guest are also welcome to use the Club's equipment for badminton, volleyball, croquet, horseshoes, soccer and baseball. Also popular with many guests are the hunting and fishing opportunities. Outfitting and guide services are available for most outdoor activities, so inquire for referrals.

How to get there: From the Northeast and East (Philadelphia and Washington): From I-81 South to Route 33 (Harrisonburg exit). Take Route 33 west 57 miles to Route 28 south at Judy Gap, WV. Take Route 28 south 22 miles to Route 250 near Durbin. From Durbin go to 250/92 north 9.5 miles to the Cheat Mountain Club access road. From the Southwest and Northwest (Charleston and Pittsburgh): Take I-79 to Weston exit 99. Take Route 33 east to Elkins. Take Route 250/

219 south to Huttonsville. Take Route 250/92south 13 miles to the CMC access road.

Innkeeper: Sherry Wates.

Address/Telephone: P. O. Box 28, Durbin, WV 26264, 304-456-4627, fax 304-456-3192.

Web page: wvweb.com/www/cheat_mtn_club/

E-mail: cheatmc@neumedia.net

Rooms: 10, all with shared bath except the suite. Smoking in designated areas. Children welcome; call about pets.

Rates: $ 80. to 150.; includes three home cooked meals daily. Accept Visa, Mastercard, cash, and check.

Open: Year around. Facilities and activities: Lodge offers full outfitting service. Available nearby are fishing, hiking, mountain biking, cross country skiing.

Facilities and activities: Lodge offers full outfitting service. Available nearby are fishing, hiking, mountain biking, and cross country skiing.

ELKINS

The Graceland Inn and Conference Center

Poised on a hill above the lovely college town of Elkins sits the majestic Graceland Inn and Conference Center. The Inn was built in 1893 by Senator Henry Gassaway Davis, a West Virginia coal and railroad baron. The Inn is a splendid example of Queen Anne architecture, and is built of native sandstone and hardwoods. Originally Davis called the house Mingo Moor, but renamed it for his youngest daughter, Grace. Next door is the equally grand mansion called Halliehurst, for another of the senator's daughters. The two mansions, along with the ice house and estate gate house, form a National Historic District.

Entering Graceland's Great Hall – 60 feet long and two stories high

– guests are greeted by enormous stained and leaded glass windows, a massive fireplace, and a 15 foot mural of Blackwater Falls. Native woods used for interior paneling and woodwork include cherry, walnut, and bird's eye maple. A broad staircase leads to an open balcony and guest rooms on the second and third floors.

There are 13 distinctive guest rooms at Graceland, all furnished with antiques. Each room also includes a private bath, an individual climate control, and access for computers. For special occasions, there are three beautiful suites in the Inn. Senator Davis' Suite is located in the southwest turret of the house, with an octagonal bedroom, a sitting room with a sleep sofa, a two person shower, and a view of the valley below. The Ellen Bruce Lee Suite also has a view of the valley, as well as a canopy bed, marble top tub, and a sleep sofa in its sitting room. Grace's Suite is located on the third floor in the southwest turret. The octagonal bedroom has a canopy bed and a panoramic view of the beautiful Tygart Valley below. The suite also has a sitting room.

Graceland offers fine dining, including dinner and Sunday brunch, in the Mingo Room. Guests at the Inn are served a continental breakfast in the Mingo Room or on the verandah.

Adjacent to the Inn is the Robert C. Byrd Center for Hospitality & Tourism. With meeting space for up to 100 people, it is the ideal location for executive retreats, meetings, and small conferences. The center has 26 recently remodeled guest rooms, all with private baths and queen size beds. Two of the rooms are equipped for disabled visitors.

Besides numerous sporting activities in the area, guests can enjoy the local Civil War sites, antique and specialty shops, and restaurants. The area also boasts fairs and festivals from March through October.

How to get there: From I-79, take Route 33 east to Elkins. As you enter Elkins, Route 33 and Route 219 intersect; turn left (north) onto Route 219 towards Parsons. Immediately on your right is a service road which takes you up a hill to Graceland.

Innkeeper: Dick Flack

*Address/Telephone:*100 Campus Drive, Elkins, WV 26241, 304-637-1600/800-624-3157, fax 304-637-1809.

Web page: wvweb.com/GRACELAND

E-mail: graceland@dnc.wvnet.edu

Rooms: 13 rooms, all with private baths. Sorry, no pets or smoking. Children welcome.

Rates: $ 77. - 180. in the Inn, includes continental breakfast; $ 57. or $ 72. in the conference center. Accept Mastercard, Visa, American Express and Discover.

Open: Year around.

Facilities and activities: Conference Center with meeting space for up to 100 people. Swimming and tennis available at nearby Davis & Elkins College. Nearby recreation areas: Monongahela National Forest, Canaan Valley State Park, Blackwater Falls State Park, and three ski areas. Other outdoor opportunities include mountain biking, hiking, hunting, fishing, camping, caving, rock climbing, canoeing and kayaking.

The Post House Bed & Breakfast

Nestled in the heart of the mountains, the Post House Bed & Breakfast is surrounded with beautiful views. With Post House located near Davis & Elkins College, guests can enjoy many local cultural activities, including the Augusta Heritage Festival held annually at the College.

Post House was built from the hardwood forests in the area. The wooden parts of the house are all of formerly indigenous hardwoods; the furniture in the house is made of cherry, black walnut, and curly maple. The house was built in the early 1930s by Clyde Post. The Clyde Post family resided in the house until 1993, when Clyde's wife, Bertha Post, died in the house at age 97.

For those wanting rooms with a private bath, guests can choose from two different options. The master guest room is furnished with beautiful black walnut furniture. For those with children, choose the charming country bedroom, which has an adjoining play room with twin beds.

How to get there: From I-81 or I-78, take Route 33 into Elkins; from the North take Route 219. Follow Harrison Avenue to Robert E. Lee Avenue.

Innkeeper: JoAnn Post Barlow

Address/Telephone: 306 Robert E. Lee Avenue, Elkins, WV 26241, 304-636-1792.

Web page: www.virtualcities.com/ons/wv/z/wvz7603.htm

E-mail: jabarlow@juno.com

Rooms: 2 with private bath; 3 with shared bath. Children welcome; sorry no pets or smoking. Check out is at 11 a.m.

Rates: $ 60. - 65. Cash or personal check only.

Open: July through October.

Facilities and activities: On premises: Large porch, backyard with playhouse for children, massage available, quilts for sale. Nearby are state parks and national forests for innumerable outdoor activities. Nearby attractions include the Monongahela National Forest,

Blackwater Falls, and Seneca Rocks. At these and other area spots there are plenty of opportunities for biking, hiking, skiing, hunting, and fishing.

The Retreat Bed & Breakfast

The Retreat Bed & Breakfast is located in a stately home that celebrated its centennial in 1996. The Retreat is located close to the campus of Davis & Elkins College, within easy walking distance of downtown Elkins, and close to the majestic, 840,000 acre Monongahela National Forest. The Retreat opened in 1987 as a mountain country inn. A perfect place to enjoy the arts in the summer, brilliant foliage in autumn, and spectacular wintry scenes, your host at The Retreat, Leslie Henderson, looks forward to your visit.

The first occupants of the house, the family of Major Joseph French and Luceba Elizabeth Harding, gave the house its name. History buffs may be interested to know that Major Harding is said to have fired the last shot of the Civil War. The Retreat remained in the Harding family until 1959 when it was sold. It was purchased in 1986 for its current use as a bed and breakfast.

Your stay at the Retreat includes a full breakfast, usually featuring homemade baked goods, seasonal fruits, and special coffees and tea. Special dietary needs can be accommodated with sufficient notice. Perhaps the most unique and informative part of your stay at the Retreat, and in the Elkins area, is the opportunity to spend time with Leslie Henderson, the Retreat's owner. Leslie has a Master's degree in Forestry, and is an avid biker, hiker, and skier. Obviously, she can give you directions to the best spots in the Forest and the region for enjoying these activities. For those a little less athletically inclined, she also knows where the wildflowers are, where to find cranberries, and where to take a leisurely stroll. Having supported herself for many years as a weaver, basket maker, and gourmet cook, she can also offer tips for those wishing to learn about local craft opportunities. The biggest of these is the local Augusta Heritage Festival held each summer at Davis & Elkins. Having been involved with the Festival for over 16 years, Leslie can take care of all your needs and questions regarding the Festival.

How to get there: Enter Elkins on U.S. 33 or U.S. 219/250. These highways use Randolph Avenue through Elkins. On Randolph Avenue, about halfway through town, is a large statue of Senator Davis on a horse (on your left if traveling east, your right if traveling west). Turn at the statue onto Sycamore Street, which becomes Harpertown Road. The Retreat is about .6 mile from the statue on your right at 214 Harpertown Road.

Innkeeper: Leslie Henderson

Address/Telephone: 214 Harpertown Road, Elkins, WV 26241, 304-636-2960/888-636-2960.

Web page: http://wvweb.com/www/retreat/index.html

E-mail: retreat@neumedia.net

Rooms: 5, 4 with shared baths; 1 with private bath. Sorry, no smoking or pets. Children welcome on restricted basis; please call to make arrangements.

Rates: $ 50. single to $ 80. double occupancy; includes full breakfast. Accept Visa, Mastercard, personal checks.

Open: Year around.

Facilities and activities: Nearby are the Monongahela National Forest and 3 major ski resorts. Tennis, hiking, mountain biking, rock climbing, swimming, skiing, golf and all mountain sports are available close by.

Tunnel Mountain Bed & Breakfast

Tunnel Mountain Bed & Breakfast is a 60-year old house made of local country fieldstone, nestled under lovely shade trees on the side of Tunnel Mountain. The house was built by a local car dealer in the 1930s, who used interesting woods in its construction, such as rare wormy chestnut and knotty pine. Your hosts Anne and Paul Beardslee have filled the house with lots of antiques and handmade crafts, and will immediately make you feel at home. Both Anne and Paul previously worked as Admissions Directors at small colleges, and are now thoroughly enjoying their new profession as innkeepers. Their bed and breakfast offers five private, wooded acres, which are surrounded by beautiful mountain peaks, lush forests, and sparkling rivers. Dog lovers can enjoy the company of the hosts' two lovable golden retrievers. Visitors from the city may marvel at the deer grazing unafraid in the back yard; as many as 23 deer have been seen at one time there.

The three romantic guest rooms all have private baths, sensational views, and lovely antiques. Guests choose from the pre-Civil War canopy bed guest room, the snug antique rope bed guest room, or the cozy third floor wormy chestnut paneled suite, which has a queen size bed and a sitting area. A full breakfast is served between 8 and 9:30 a.m. Guests eat at an antique dining table in a setting complete with rare tools, country curios, and antiques. Dishes served include stuffed French toast and apple cinnamon pancakes. During the five weeks of the Augusta Heritage Festival in July and August, your hosts serve a continental breakfast. Special dietary needs can be accommodated with sufficient notice.

Elkins is the home of Davis & Elkins College, the annual Augusta Arts & Crafts Workshops and Festival, and the annual Mountain State Forest Festival. An annual Ramp Festival and Cook-off is held in the spring. Outdoor enthusiasts will want to visit nearby Monongahela National Forest for hiking, cross country skiing, or mountain biking. Also located nearby are Blackwater Falls and Canaan Valley State Parks, Dolly Sods, Seneca Rocks, and Spruce Knob. Elkins also has historic sites, antique and craft shops, and restaurants.

How to get there: Located 4 miles east of Elkins. Take the Stuart Recreation Exit (Old Route 33) off Route 33 and continue .2 mile. Look for the sign on the left side of the road.

Innkeepers: Anne and Paul Beardslee

Address/Telephone: Route 1, Box 59-1, Elkins, WV 26241, 304-636-1684. 888-211-9123

Web page: www.virtualcities.com/ons/wv/z/wvz3601.htm

Rooms: 3, all with private baths. Children welcome over 13; sorry, no pets. Smoking in restricted areas only.

Rates: $ 65. - 75.; includes full breakfast. Discounts for AARP, Augusta Students, and stays more than 5 nights. Credit cards not accepted.

Open: Year around.

Facilities and Activities: Nearby are hiking, fishing, rock climbing, hunting, skiing, golf, swimming, and mountain biking. Also located nearby are Blackwater Falls and Canaan Valley State Parks, Dolly Sods, Seneca Rocks, Spruce Knob, Monongahela National Forest, and historic downtown Elkins. Several state festivals are held annually in the area.

Warfield House

Warfield House is a grand "Old Colonies Style" house adjacent to Davis & Elkins College. Built around 1901, the house features spectacular stained glass, an ornate staircase and molding, and an enormous terra cotta fireplace. The house was built during the boom days of Elkins when the West Virginia Central and Pittsburgh Railroad Company was in operation. The railroad's founders, Senator Henry Gassaway Davis and Senator Stephen Benton Elkins, brought the railroad to this valley because of its abundant coal and timber.

Guests at Warfield House can choose from five different guest rooms. The Oak Room has a high backed oak bed and a whirlpool bath. The Pine Room has two double iron beds and a shared bath. The Walnut Room has a Victorian walnut double bed and a private bath. The Maple Room has an 1830 canopy plantation bed with a shared bath.

The Nest Room has a double bed and a private bath with a claw foot tub. Whether you are enjoying the morning sun in the Maple Room's bay window or relaxing on the wraparound front porch, guests at Warfield House are peaceably relaxed.

How to get there: From Pittsburgh or Charleston: Follow I-79 to Weston/Buckhannon Exit 99. Take Route 33 East into Elkins. Turn left at the Iron Horse Statue. B & B is located across from City Park and adjacent to Davis & Elkins College.

Innkeepers: Connie and Paul Garnett

Address/Telephone: 318 Buffalo Street, Elkins, WV 26241, 304-636-4555/888-636-4555, fax 304-636-1457.

Web page: www.virtualcities.com/ons/wv/z/wvz7602.htm

Rooms: 5, with private and shared baths. Sorry, no smoking, pets, or children under 12. Check out is 11 a.m.

Rates: $ 65. - 85. per night double occupancy; includes full breakfast. Accept cash, check, or traveler's checks.

Open: Year around.

Facilities and activities: Guest refrigerator, bicycles, and wraparound porch. Located five minutes from downtown with restaurants, shops, and theaters. Golf and tennis are nearby. Hiking, mountain biking and other sports abound in the surrounding state parks and forests.

HELVETIA

The Beekeeper Inn

The Beekeeper Inn is nestled in the beautiful mountains of Randolph County in the charming village of Helvetia. A magical place with tall firs and mountain streams, the Inn is one of the oldest buildings in Helvetia. The Beekeeper Inn was built around 1870, and was the home of the town's original beekeeper.

The Inn itself is filled with antiques, and has three comfortable bedrooms for guests, each with a private bath. Guests can also enjoy the book-filled common room, small kitchen, and breezy outdoor deck. Visitors to the Inn often stroll the shaded country roads, fish in the stream, or lie in the hammock under the pines. For more active pursuits, the Inn is located 15 miles from Holly River State Park, 20 miles from the West Virginia State Game Preserve, and 12 miles from Kumbrabow State Forest.

Visitors are encouraged to check out the delicious food at the nearby Hutte Restaurant. The Hutte is open every day from noon until 7:00 p.m., and has a full menu. Sunday features a country brunch called *Bernerplatte*, truly a Swiss delight.

How to get there: Take I-79 to Buckhannon. Then take Route 20 South to French Creek. Next take Route 46 to Helvetia. From Elkins, take Route 250 South, turn right at Mill Creek. Travel Route 46 to Helvetia.

Innkeeper: Eleanor F. Mailloux

Address/Telephone: Helvetia, WV 26224, 304-924-6435.

Rooms: 3, all with private bath. Smoking and children over 6 permitted. Pets allowed in penthouse.

Rates: $ 60. single occupancy; $ 85. double; includes full breakfast. Check or cash only.

Open: Year around.

Facilities/Activities: Mountain biking, hiking, and outdoor activities at nearby Holly River State Park and Kumbrabow State Forest.

HILLSBORO

The Current Bed and Breakfast

For persons wanting to explore the Greenbrier River Trail, the Current Bed and Breakfast is the place to stay. This 1905 Victorian farmhouse, built by the Beard family and now owned by Leslee McCarty, is located almost as close to the trail as you can get. In addition to the pleasures of the trail, the Current has many other enticements: good food, beautiful views, and comfortable rooms. Guests usually enjoy time spent outdoors, relaxing on the screened porch or in the outdoor hot tub, all while admiring Leslee's gardens and, again, the lovely surrounding hills and valleys.

The Current has five comfortable guest rooms, all of which share 2 and a half baths. There is also a suite, which has a private bath and a sitting room. All the rooms in the farmhouse are furnished with period antiques. Guests will enjoy looking at Leslee's quilt and doll collections, as well as the spectacular views of the river valley.

How to get there: Take Route 219 from Hillsboro, turn on Denmar Road. Travel five miles, following signs to the Greenbrier River Trail. The Current is located at the intersection of Denmar Road and Beard Post Office Road.

Innkeeper: Leslee McCarty

Address/Telephone: HC 64, Box 135, Hillsboro, WV 24946, 304-653-4722.

Web page: www.carrwebb.com/thecurrent

E-mail: current@inetone.net

Rooms: 5 rooms share $2\frac{1}{2}$ baths; the suite has private bath. Children welcome. Inquire about pets. Sorry, no smoking.

Rates: $ 45. single occupancy; $ 60. double; $ 85. for suite with private bath. All include full breakfast. Dinners by prior arrangement. Accept Mastercard, Visa, cash and check.

Open: Year around.

Facilities and activities: Outdoor hot tub and screened porch. Located immediately on the 80 mile Greenbrier River Trail, suitable for hiking, biking, and horseback riding. Nearby are Beartown, Watoga State Park, Cranberry Wilderness Botanical Area, and Pearl Buck Birthplace.

HUNTERSVILLE

Carriage House Inn Bed & Breakfast

The Carriage House Inn, circa 1852, is a fine example of 19th century architecture, and is located in Huntersville, West Virginia. Huntersville was originally the home of the county seat, until the seat was moved to Marlinton, six miles away. The Carriage House Inn was used during the Civil War as a temporary hospital. The five bedrooms of the Inn have been thoughtfully restored with private baths and other comforts. Enjoy your host Jeanne Dunham's tempting breakfasts, and sit by the cozy wood stove in the dining room. Games and books are available for relaxing in the living room, on the front porch, or in your room. You might enjoy saying hello to Jeanne's sweet dogs, Pepper, Bear and Maggie.

Jeanne can direct you to local festivals and other goings on in the area. Country crafts and homemade goodies are available, and guests can make arrangements to have lunch or dinner at the Inn. The Carriage House Inn Gift Shop is located in the renovated barn, which is attached to the Inn. The shop offers a wide variety of arts and crafts created by more than 100 West Virginia artists. Jeanne has also opened "The Christmas Corner" shop, also located on the property.

There is no shortage of outdoor activities in the area to keep you busy. Nearby is Watoga State Park, with hiking trails, swimming, and lake fishing. Cranberry Glades demonstrates a slice of the Arctic left over from the Ice Age. Civil War buffs will want to visit nearby Droop Mountain Battlefield Park. Nearby Marlinton offers shopping, a golf course, a county museum, and access to the Greenbrier River Trail, for hiking, biking, cross country skiing, or horseback riding. In Hillsboro, visitors may tour the beautifully restored birthplace of Nobel Prize winner, Pearl S. Buck.

How to get there: From Marlinton, take Route 39 six miles to Huntersville.

Innkeepers: Jeanne M. Dunham

Address/Telephone: HCR 82, Box 56, Huntersville, WV 24954, 304-799-6706.

Web page: http://wvweb.com/www/carriage_house/web.htm/

Rooms: 5, and one suite, all with private baths. Children welcome;

sorry, no pets. Absolutely no smoking.

Rates: $ 55. - 100. per night depending on season; includes full breakfast. Accept Visa, Mastercard, cash, or check.

Open: Year around, except Thanksgiving and Christmas.

Facilities and activities: Two gift shops on premises. Meals besides breakfast can be arranged. Nearby state parks with hiking, swimming, and fishing. Located 6 miles from Marlinton with shopping, restaurants, and the Greenbrier River Trail. At nearby Snowshoe Resort, try the skiing, mountain biking, swimming, tennis, or golf.

HUTTONSVILLE

The Cardinal Inn

Guests coming to the Cardinal Inn are struck by their first glimpse of the grounds, with the Inn perched at the top of a hill. If you take a moment to relax on the large front porch, the view is also incredible. As a matter of fact, the view is good from every room in the house. The house itself is located on 75 acres, which guests can use for biking or hiking. Visitors can hunt on the property if they obtain a Westvaco hunting permit (Westvaco property borders the Cardinal Inn property.)

Originally there was a red brick Colonial house on the site where the current house stands. The Colonial structure burnt to the ground in 1901, and Colonel Hutton promptly built the present house. While the early nineteenth century house is gone, there are several historic outbuildings on the property. The building originally housing the blacksmith shop is still standing, and is dated 1808. One of the other colonial outbuildings has been leased to the owners of a successful outdoor guide business, for which there is a great demand in the area.

When you step inside the Inn, you will meet your hostess, Eunice Kwasniewski, and her two charming cats: Flubber and Wringer. Flubber and Wringer are brother and sister. Usually Wringer doesn't budge from the warmth of the VCR, but will sometimes show off for guests by doing a tightrope act on the stair rail. Observing Wringer on the stair rail, you may notice that all of the lovely woodwork and cabinets in the house are oak.

There are nine guest rooms for rent at the Cardinal Inn. Some of the guests rooms have private baths; three of the guest rooms have sinks in the room. At one time Colonel Hutton had a handicapped relative who lived in one of the second floor front rooms. She rarely left her bedroom and sitting room, but did live to be 100 years old. One of the other guest rooms is called the Crazy Room. No, a wacky relative did not reside here. Instead the room was named for its odd shape, which is due to it being built with three chimneys going through the center of the room. Because of the shape of the house, several of the guest rooms have unusual wall and window configurations, always resulting in lovely bows and interesting rooms. There is even a romantic turret room. The Inn's 66 windows made furnishing the house with storm windows quite an undertaking. Mrs. Kwasniewski can still recall the electricians' frustration caused by the house's solid brick walls: a real challenge when replacing the wiring.

On the lovely front grounds of the Inn, many a wedding has been held, oftentimes with the vows being exchanged inside the large gazebo. The Inn frequently plays host to weddings, receptions, and other large events like family reunions. To make things simple, the owner's daughter has a catering service, and the Inn already has the large tents often requested for outdoor events. Consider the Cardinal Inn for your next family occasion, or perhaps just a lovely night's stay.

How to get there: Take Route 33 into Elkins. Turn left at Route 219/250 and travel about 17 miles; turn right at Route 219. The Cardinal Inn is approximately .5 mile down 219.

Innkeeper: Eunice Kwasniewski

Address/Telephone: Route 1, Box 1, Route 219, Huttonsville, WV 26273, 304-335-6149/800-335-6149.

Web page: www.virtualcities.com/ons/wv/a/wvaa702.htm.

Rooms: Nine, all with shared baths. Sorry, no smoking or pets. Children welcome.

Rates: $ 40. single occupancy; $ 55. double; includes breakfast. Accept Mastercard and Visa.

Open: Year around.

Facilities and activities: Reservations can be made for lunches, brunches, and dinners for parties of six or more. Are equipped for large special events. Located close to Snowshoe, Silver Creek, and Canaan Valley Ski Resorts. Large gazebo on grounds available for musical performances and receptions.

Hutton House

1998 marked the 100 year anniversary of the charming Hutton House, so schedule a visit to this centegenarian. Hutton House, located in Huttonsville, is on the National Register of Historic Places. The house is a large, yellow, three-story, Queen Anne Victorian, set high on a hill. Up at the house, guests will enjoy beautiful views and well-tended grounds with cheery flower gardens. You can enjoy all this from one of the several inviting porches. As you walk through the grounds, you may hear the tree swing calling your name, where you can sit and watch the black and white kitty sunning herself in the garden.

I love the story of how the current owners, Loretta Murray and Dean Ahren, acquired the property. Loretta and Dean were engaged to be married, with an agreement that they would remain in the college town of Skidmore, Pennsylvania, after their union. (The best laid plans. . . . .) They came to West Virginia on their honeymoon, and loving old houses, offhandedly took a look at Hutton House, which was for sale. After a few late night discussions and several drinks, they decided to buy the place. The business is well-suited for Loretta and her lucky guests, as she loves to cook and fixes big gourmet breakfasts for guests. Sometimes early-bird skiers request a little more plain fare, and she is happy to oblige. Breakfast for the non-early birds and big breakfast eaters is prepared whenever you wake up and wander downstairs. Loretta usually alternates between what she calls a "sweet day" and a "savory day." A typical sweet day might include French toast stuffed with apricot jam and cream cheese. A savory day might include zucchini pancakes topped with a poached egg and sun-dried tomato sauce.

Old house buffs will appreciate the beautiful woodwork running throughout the house, as well as the original colored tiles surrounding the fireplaces. Loretta has spent a lot of time and thought decorating the house — each guest room has a cohesive decor, and all the windows have decorative Victorian panes at the top. There are six guest rooms for rent. Three are on the second floor and three are on the third. All have private baths. Loretta says she likes her guests to feel at home during their stay at Hutton House, and particularly likes when they hang out with her in the kitchen, which happens frequently.

The average guest at Hutton House is usually a skier, mountain biker, or person on a vacation or romantic getaway. They do have one very regular guest who has stayed with them over 40 times. This particular guest rides his motorcycle all over the country, and has found Hutton House to be one of his favorite places to stay. Loretta and Dean offer a fly fishing course, and there are also plenty of other outdoor activities available nearby. On the other hand, I might just choose to relax on the front porch after filling my belly with French toast or pancakes.

How to get there: Located seventeen miles south of Elkins on Routes 250 and 219 in Huttonsville.

Innkeeper: Loretta Murray and Dean Ahren

Address/Telephone: Routes 250 & 219, P. O. Box 88, Huttonsville, WV 26273, 304-335-6701/800-234-6701.

Web page: www.wvonline.com/shareourbeds/hutton/

E-mail: hutton@citynet.net

Rooms: 6, all with private bath. Children are welcome. Sorry, no pets or smoking.

Rates: $ 75. per night; includes full gourmet breakfast. Accept cash, check, Mastercard or Visa.

Open: Year around.

Facilities and activities: Guests can enjoy the entire house, including the television room, large wraparound porch, deck and gardens. Located within an hour of Snowshoe and Canaan Ski Resorts, mountain biking, national forests, Seneca Rocks, Spruce Knob, and the charming towns of Helvetia and Elkins.

The Linger In

The Linger In is a vacation retreat located in a renovated turn-of-the-century farmhouse. The house overlooks the picturesque Tygart Valley and the small town of Huttonsville. The Inn operates as an "unhosted" vacation rental property, with your hostess Betty Linger residing across the street. The Linger In is rented by the week, or for two or more nights, by one family or a group of friends. Having the entire house to yourselves, you will enjoy a relaxing vacation in a tranquil setting.

One of the foremost spots to relax is outside next to the Inn's swimming pool. For more active outdoor pursuits, take a hike through the woods to the top of the mountain, or take a look around the working dairy farm, and help feed baby calves. Some guests enjoy a walk or bike ride through the farm roads and along the Tygart Valley River. Also in the area are numerous restaurants, antique and gift shops, and Snowshoe and Silver Creek ski resorts.

There are six bedrooms to choose from, each furnished with antiques and country charm. One bedroom has a queen size bed, three have full size beds, one has a king and a twin bed, and one has a twin only. Visitors share two newly remodeled bathrooms. Guests can cook meals in a truly modern country kitchen, and eat at an old country table in the kitchen, in the large dining room, or outside on the picnic table.

How to get there: From Charleston, take I-79 to the Weston/Buckhannon exit, Exit 99. Take Route 33 east to Elkins. At Elkins take Route 250 south to Huttonsville. From Washington, D.C., follow I-66 west to Strasburg, VA. Take I-81 south, then follow Route 55 west to Seneca Rocks, and turn right on Route 33 west to Elkins. At Elkins take Route 250 to Huttonsville.

Innkeepers: Betty and Russell Linger

Address/Telephone: P. O. Box 14, Huttonsville, WV 26273, 304-335-4434/800-422-3304.

Web page: http://www.wvonline.com/shareourbeds/linger_in.

Rooms: Rent entire house, with 6 bedrooms, sharing two baths. Children welcome. Sorry, no smoking or pets.

Rates: For two persons, $ 100. for a minimum stay of two nights, $500. for a week. Accept personal check or cash.

Open: Year around.

Facilities and activities: Furnished house with television and VCR. Enjoy hiking on property and visit working dairy farm. Nearby are ski resorts, antique shops, auctions, and fly fishing.

Mr. Richard's Country Inn

Mr. Richard's Country Inn is located in a pre-Civil War mansion, built in 1835. Much of the Inn is filled with lovely antiques. If interested in historic houses, have your host, Richard Brown, tell you about the many beautiful woods represented in the woodwork and mantles of the different rooms. Ask to see the beautiful chestnut woodwork in the house; something now rarely seen after the chestnut blight.

Richard lives at the Inn with his four happy dogs. In the mornings, you may see Richard crossing the beautiful grounds behind the Inn, among large willow, pine, and hemlock trees, with four pups trailing ahead or behind him. Retired from the Justice Department, Richard opened the Inn and cozily filled it with family heirlooms, antiques, and a few odds and ends. There are thirteen guest rooms at the Inn, most with private baths, and some with wood burning fireplaces. The rooms in the older section of the house are more spacious and filled with antiques; antique-lovers should request one of those rooms.

As you arrive at the Inn, you will see a large verandah across the front of the house, usually filled with guests relaxing or eating. From the verandah, you can enjoy lovely mountain and valley views, with peaceful cornfields, including deer nibbling the crop. The Inn has a full restaurant and a large bar. Entree choices include steaks, pan-fried rainbow trout, ham, fried chicken, and chicken pecan. The restaurant, bar, and music make for a friendly and fun dining atmosphere.

Mr. Richards' maintains a slightly eclectic clientele, with many repeat customers and friends dropping in. Staying at the Inn while we were there was an author writing a fly-fishing book, and two guests arriving on huge Harley-Davidsons. The guests were very friendly, and a group was planning to go into town that evening for some late night dancing. Your host has many interesting stories to tell about both the Inn and the history of the region.

How to get there: Located on Route 219, the Inn is 22 miles south of Elkins, and 20 miles north of Snowshoe.

Innkeeper: Richard Brown

Address/Telephone: Route 1, Box 11-A-1, Huttonsville, WV 26273, 304-335-6659/800-636-7434.

Web page: www.virtualcities.com/ons/wv/h/wvh19010.htm

E-mail: lvargas@neumedia.net

Rooms: 13, 9 with private bath. Children welcome; call about pets. Smoking allowed in some rooms.

Rates: $ 60. - 85. double occupancy; includes full breakfast. Accept Mastercard, Visa, and American Express.

Open: Year around.

Facilities and activities: Close to town of Elkins. Many outdoor activities available in nearby state parks and national forests, including mountain biking, caving, hiking, skiing, fly fishing, canoeing, white water rafting. Golf available at nearby Snowshoe Resort. There is antique shopping in the area, as well as the Cass Scenic Railroad.

MARLINTON

The Jerico Inn and Bed and Breakfast

You approach the charming Jerico Inn and Bed and Breakfast down a gravel drive, and find it nestled in the woods. There's a good chance a sweet-natured retriever, wrongly named Worthless, will be lying on the side porch wagging his tail when you drive up. The friendly innkeeper will also greet you, and make you feel right at home. The Inn's owner is Tom Moore, a very talented gentleman who has done all of the renovation around the place. This includes renovating the old farm house with its five guest rooms, as well as moving and rebuilding six log cabins on the property. At the turn of the century, Tom's family owned the property and built the main house. Eventually the house and property were sold, and subsequently were used as rental property. By the time Tom was able to purchase the property, the house had fallen into such disrepair that all the windows had been knocked out. Tom has had his work cut out for him, but has done a wonderful and inventive job, making the Jerico a charming and unique place to stay. Giving testament to this fact are its guests who come from all over the country. The Jerico has also developed a following among some writers and politicians from the D.C. area. After visiting the Jerico, I can see why it would be the perfect place for a writer to hole up and work . . . or maybe just relax and get inspired.

Breakfast is included for guests staying in one of the guest rooms in the main house; there is a small charge of $ 5. for breakfast for guests staying in the cabins. All of the guest rooms in the main house have a private bath and a television in the room. Some of the rooms have air conditioning, but it is rarely needed in this part of the state. There is a charming upstairs porch where you can look out on the surrounding woodlands. Guests are welcome to use the Inn's refrigerator for cold drinks or snacks. Often you'll find visitors hanging out in the cozy family room, which has a TV, VCR, checkerboard and other games. There is also a hot tub for guests' use.

Enjoying a slightly rustic retreat, it is hard for me to imagine a more romantic place to stay than in one of the Jerico's six log cabins. Tom was granted permission to remove the cabins from nearby Droop Mountain, a Civil War battlefield. When re-building the cabins on his property several years ago, Tom added lots of wonderful touches and amenities, including gorgeous hand hewn beams. He also added picturesque porches, one of which overlooks a gurgling stream. Three of the cabins have private hot tubs. Those without private tubs can use the Inn's main hot tub.

All of the cabins are decorated with quaint country antiques and furnishings. The blue cabin overlooks a stream and has a double bed, two twin beds, and a sofa bed; it can sleep four to six people. The cabin in the rear of the property has a private hot tub and a wood burning stove. It has one bedroom downstairs, as well as a loft bedroom upstairs. The "Honeymoon Cabin" has a stained glass window and inviting front porch. Several cabins can sleep 8-10 people and have 2 private bedrooms. Each cabin has a furnished kitchen and cable television.

There is a picnic table on the grounds for guests' use, as well as an outdoor grill. The Jerico is also available for wedding parties and family reunions, where families rent out the entire house and all three cabins. I can't think of a better setting for such events.

How to get there: From Route 219 just south of Marlinton, turn onto Jerico Road at the sign for the Inn. You will soon come to the Inn, sitting up on a small hill.

Owner: Tom Moore

Address/Telephone: Jerico Road, Marlinton, WV 24954, 304-799-6241.

Web page: http://wvweb.com/www/jerico_bb/web.html

Rooms: 6, all with private bath; also 6 cabins for rent. Well-trained pets allowed in some cabins only. Sorry, no smoking.

Rates: Main house, $ 35. - 65. a night; includes full breakfast. Cabins are $ 65. - 150.; cabin guests pay $5. for breakfast, if desired. Discounts available for extended stays.

Open: Year around.

Facilities and activities: On the property are hot tubs, a picnic table and grill. The Inn is located in close proximity to many outdoor activities, including: mountain biking, downhill and cross country skiing, fly fishing, and hiking. Restaurants and shopping available in nearby Marlinton and Hillsboro. Marlinton is located on the Greenbrier River Trail.

MOOREFIELD

McMechen House Inn

Try to schedule a visit to the lovely McMechen House Inn, cradled in the historic South Branch Valley, surrounded by the majestic mountains of the Potomac Highlands. A peaceful and pristine part of the state, the valley was the site of fierce struggle during the Civil War. The house itself was built in 1853 by Samuel A. McMechen, a local merchant and political activist. During the Civil War, McMechen House served as headquarters to both the Union and Confederate forces. It is now on the National Register of Historic Places.

The three-story brick Greek Revival home, located in the center of Moorefield's historic district, is full of surprises and steeped in 19th century romance. Guests can read a family will that disinherits a daughter for marrying against her father's wishes, or marvel at 150-year old political slogans painted on the wall of one room.

A stay at McMechen House includes breakfast as well as afternoon tea. Breakfast is served in the formal dining room where, in winter, a cast-iron Ben Franklin stove keeps the room warm and cozy. From Mother's Day through November, guests and other visitors can enjoy lunch and dinner at the Green Shutters Garden Café, located on the premises. During the other months of the year, guests can make arrangements with their hosts to have lunch or dinner prepared for them.

The Inn has five regular rooms from which guests can choose. The largest offering is the McCoy Suite. It has a double bed, parlor, and private bath. Carrie's Room has a double bed, private bath, and a small refrigerator in the room. Both Elizabeth's and Emma's Rooms have two double beds and a private bath. The Buchanan Room has a double bed with a shared bath. If all of these rooms are rented, other rooms are available.

Guests will enjoy the Antique, Book, and Gift Shop located at McMechen House. In the shop you'll find treasures such as antiques, linens, china, pottery, and work by local artists and craftspeople. Before or after shopping, guests often like to relax on the spacious porches at the Inn.

Several times a year, innkeeper/actor Bob Curtis presents "The Story of W. H. Maloney," a one-man play describing a Confederate private's experiences in the area during the Civil War. With sufficient notice, the Curtises can arrange for tours of Civil War battle sites. Other area attractions include Lost River State Park, Seneca Rocks, tours of several area wineries, the Potomac Eagle excursion train, canoeing, fishing, and kayaking. In town, there is a walking tour of the Moorefield Historic District and an active community theater.

How to get there: The Inn is located at the intersection of Route 55 and Route 220 in Moorefield, WV.

Innkeepers: Bob and Linda Curtis

Address/Telephone: 109 North Main Street, Moorefield, WV 26836, 304-538-7173/800-298-2466, fax 304-538-7841.

Web page: www.virtualcities.com/ons/wv/z/wvz5801.htm

Rooms: 5 regular rooms, 4 with private bath. Other rooms are available. Sorry, no smoking or pets. Children welcome.

Rates: $ 75. - 125. single or double occupancy; includes breakfast and afternoon tea. Accept most major credit cards.

Open: Year around

Facilities and activities: On premises: Green Shutter Garden Café, open Mother's Day through October; also The McMechen House

Antique, Book & Gift Shop. Nearby: historic tours, wineries, fishing, canoeing, kayaking, golf, Seneca Rocks and Lost River State Park.

MONTROSE

White Oak Bed & Breakfast

Visit White Oak Bed & Breakfast in Montrose and make yourself at home with Isobel and Worlie Simmons. This is one of only two B & B's in West Virginia (that we know of) where you can get your hair cut: downstairs Worlie operates a small barber shop. The original house was built in 1912, with additional rooms added later. The Simmons purchased the home and surrounding property from the original owners in 1957.

A trip to White Oak would not be complete without a trip to the backyard to see the largest White Oak tree on record in West Virginia; it is indeed a magnificent sight. The tree stands 77 feet tall, and has a circumference of 18 feet, 4 inches. It really is beautiful.

Visitors to White Oak stay in a guest suite, which consists of a bedroom, private bath, large living room, and built-in kitchen. Guests have a private entrance to the game room, which contains a television, pool table, and fireplace. There is plenty of room for relaxing, if hiking on the 100 acre property wears you out. Guests can eat breakfast at the family table for a $ 3.00 additional charge; you can have a continental breakfast in your room for a $ 2.00 additional charge.

How to get there: Located in a small community called Porterwood, White Oak Bed & Breakfast is 18 miles north of Elkins on Route 219.

Innkeepers: Isobel and Worlie Simmons

Address/Telephone: Route 2, Box 112, Montrose, WV 26283, 304-478-4705

Rooms: One suite of three rooms. Children welcome; sorry, no pets or smoking. Check out 11 a.m.

Rates: $ 45. double occupancy; $ 35. single. Add nominal charge of $ 2. for continental breakfast; $ 3. for full breakfast. Personal check or cash only.

Open: Year round.

Facilities and activities: Nearby are walking, hunting, fishing, and 100 acres of White Oak forest property to explore. Home of the largest white oak in the state.

SLATYFORK

The Inn at Elk River

Pulling up to the Inn at Elk River, we were greeted by a friendly dog. It sort of summed up the atmosphere at the Inn: friendly, laid-back, and outdoorsy, with something for everyone. You cross a small section of the Elk River itself to get to the Inn. Upon your arrival you immediately see an inviting picnic table at river's edge, and beautiful mountain views beyond. Specializing in hosting mountain biking excursions, this is the perfect retreat for the outdoor enthusiast. The Inn was built in 1989, and has grown since then. It has several cozy common rooms and a full restaurant. You'll find a fireplace in the spacious dining room, and a dinner menu featuring specialties such as Fresh Elk River Tout, Fresh Broiled Salmon, Key Lime Pie and Hummingbird Cake. Guests staying in the Inn itself or the adjacent Farmhouse receive breakfast with their room, which includes homemade muffins, biscuits, pancakes, omelets and coffee. Guests in the cabins can enjoy breakfast for an additional fee. Picnic lunches are available with special biking packages.

There are 5 bedrooms for rent in the Inn, and five bedrooms for rent in the adjacent farmhouse. All the rooms have hardwood floors, are furnished with country antiques, and have beautiful views. Guests can also enjoy an outdoor hot tub. Groups or families may want to rent one of the 3 two-bedroom cabins. Each cabin has a washer and dryer, especially handy after a muddy mountain bike ride.

The Inn at Elk River is also host to "The Fat Tire Festival," a three day extravaganza held each summer for mountain bikers and their families. Most participants camp out on the grounds of the Inn, (the rooms and cabins fill up quickly), and enjoy workshops, rides, races, and other festivities, all geared around mountain biking. Recently the Inn has attracted an increasing number of fly fishermen, owing to the great fly fishing in the region. Gil Willis can assist you in planning a fly fishing trip; call for details.

How to get there: Located on Route 219 near Snowshoe.

Innkeepers: Gil and Mary Willis

Address/Telephone: Highway 219, Slatyfork, WV 26291, 304-572-3771.

Web page: www.ertc.com

E-mail: elk@neumedia.net

Rooms: 10 in the Inn, all with private bath; also offer 3 two-bed-room cabins. Children welcome; friendly pets can remain outside if leashed or tethered.

Rates: In the Inn range from $ 60.- $ 100., depending on number of persons, day and time of year. Farmhouse ranges from $ 45. - $ 70. Cabins range from $ 100. - $ 120. weekdays to $ 675. - 800. per week.

Open: April through November.

Facilities and activities: Specialize in mountain biking trips. Wonderful fly fishing available nearby. Also offer crosscountry skiing and equipment rental, as well as XC ski lessons.

VALLEY HEAD

Nakiska Chalet Bed & Breakfast

Visit the comfortable and casual, wood, stone, and glass structure which is Nakiska Chalet Bed & Breakfast. Your hosts, Joyce and Doug Cooper explain that *Nakiska* is an Indian word meaning "a place where friends gather," and invite you to do so. Located on a country road, the B & B is located near downhill and cross-country skiing, golf, hiking and biking trails, and trout fishing. If you want to relax, Nakiska Chalet offers a quiet hideaway in beautiful surroundings. Built in 1981, Nakiska Chalet is a large A-frame structure with decks, surrounded by rolling hills. There is a massive stone fireplace in the living room, which is often a popular gathering place for guests.

Nakiska Chalet has many special amenities, not the least of which are Joyce's hearty pancake breakfasts. On the premises, guests can enjoy a hot tub, sauna, sledding hill, and cross country and hiking trails. If arrangements are made ahead of time, guests can enjoy a good old-fashioned West Virginia hay ride. Watch the sunset and the stars come out, while you enjoy a cup of coffee or cocoa, and homemade desserts. Hay rides are $ 15. additional for adults, and $ 1. per year of age for children. Nakiska Chalet has three guest rooms for rent. Two rooms each have a king size bed, and share a bath. One room has a queen size and a twin bed, with a private bath.

Your hosts will be happy to show you their woodworking, as well as the twig furniture that they make from local trees. They will also be glad to give you suggestions and directions to surrounding attractions, including the Pearl Buck home, Seneca Rocks, the Highland Scenic Highway, Cass Scenic Railway, and Snowshoe and Silver Creek ski resorts.

How to get there: Driving south on Route 219 from Elkins, turn right onto Mingo Flats Road. (5 miles south of the Route 219 and Route 15 junction at Valley Head). Drive 1.7 miles, turn right onto Dry Branch Road. Nakiska Chalet is .5 mile on the right. Driving north on Route 219 from Lewisburg through Marlinton, take a sharp left onto Mingo Flats Road, .9 mile north of the Randolph County Line (23 miles north of Marlinton). Drive .8 mile, turn left onto Dry Branch Road. Nakiska Chalet is .5 mile on the right. Call for a map.

Innkeepers: Joyce and Doug Cooper

Address/Telephone: HC 73, Box 24 Valley Head, WV 26294, 304-339-6309.

Web page: wvonline.com/nakiska/

E-mail: nakiska@wvonline.com

Rooms: 3; 2 with shared bath; 1 with private bath. Includes full breakfast. Sorry, no pets or smoking. Children welcome.

Rates: $ 60. - 75. year around. Accept Mastercard, Visa, check or cash.

Open: All year.

Facilities and activities: Dinner available with advance reservations; hot tub, sauna, and large fireplace. Cross country skiing, sledding, golf, hiking and biking trails, trout fishing, Cass Scenic Railroad, Greenbrier River Trail, Cranberry Glades, fall foliage, hay rides and lots of great festivals and fairs nearby.

NEW RIVER AND GREENBRIER VALLEY

Ansted, Beaver, Fayetteville, Ghent, Lansing, Lewisburg, Pence Springs, Sandstone, Summersville, White Sulphur Springs, Winona

About the region . . .

Along the common border of Virginia and West Virginia lies an area which may be the most beautiful part of either state. From Lexington, Virginia west to Beckley, West Virginia, the land is a series of rolling hills, blue ridges, and incredible views that make it a treat to drive along Interstate 64. I'm not alone in my estimation that this is an extraordinary place and favorite getaway. One October – fall foliage season in this neck of the woods — I tried to get a room anywhere from Lewisburg to Lexington. No luck.

Two particular parts of this region that West Virginians can happily claim are the town of **Lewisburg** and the beautiful Greenbrier River. The entire town of Lewisburg is a National Register Historic District, with the county library, courthouse and several churches dating back to the late 1700s and early 1800s. The town boasts Antebellum homes, a Civil War Cemetery, the North House Museum, Carnegie Hall, antique shops, and fine — as well as fun — dining.

The Greenbrier River offers swimming and canoeing; on the adjacent Greenbrier River Trail you can hike, mountain bike, and horseback ride. You'll find several state parks, white water rafting, hunting, golfing, and skiing all plentiful in this region. For more information on the area, visit or write the Lewisburg Visitor Center, Carnegie Hall, 105 Church Street, Lewisburg, WV 24901, 304-645-1000.

While traveling in or near **White Sulphur Springs**, you may want to visit the internationally-known Greenbrier Resort Hotel. Visitors not staying at the resort may make use of the dining rooms as well as the many exclusive shops within this grand hotel, which has played host to presidents and dignitaries. The Greenbrier has a world-class golf course; call about particulars and green fees.

From Lewisburg and heading north and west are **Fayetteville** and the New River Gorge National Park, home to the world's largest steel arch bridge. The town of Fayetteville was recently voted by a national magazine to be one of the best towns in the country for outdoor recreation. The spectacular New River Gorge is attracting visitors and outdoor enthusiasts from all over the world. Try your hand at white water rafting on the New and Gauley Rivers, with a skilled guide from one of the many local outfitters. The ancient New River has been flowing for over 65 million years; only the Nile is older. The area is brimming with other outdoor opportunities, including canoeing, hiking, fishing, rock climbing and mountain biking. Adventurous types should look for "Five Dollar Frank" at the local airport, giving fly-over tours of the Gorge for only $ 5. In addition to sporting activities, Fayetteville features many historic buildings, homes and B & B's, and is attracting an increasing number of restaurants and shops. If you don't mind crowds, go to "Bridge Day" held in October each year on the New River Gorge Bridge. Daredevils can be seen skydiving off the bridge to the river below. Quite a sight, and a West Virginia tradition. Be sure to wear your walking shoes.

ANSTED

Historic Parish House Bed & Breakfast

The Historic Parish House Bed & Breakfast was built in 1904 by the local Episcopal church, The Church of the Redeemer. The church was originally built as The Mission School. The former school rooms are now used by the church as their Parish Hall. The house, currently housing the B & B, was used to house school teachers, and later the resident priest.

The house itself is a Victorian, with hardwood floors, the original four-paned windows, and tiled fireplaces. There are two guest rooms to rent in the house. One is decorated with ivy wallpaper, and the other has a rose pattern. Both rooms have air conditioning, stenciled floors, and a private bath. Both rooms have fireplaces with antique cast iron covers, although the fireplaces no longer function.

Historic Parish House is located in the heart of white water rafting country. Hiking is available at nearby Hawks Nest State Park. Guests enjoy taking the tram ride at the New River Gorge, as well as jet boat rides.

How to get there: Located on Route 60 West, about six miles from Route 19.

Innkeepers: Jane Crist and Rosalie Marshall

Address/Telephone: 102 Main Street, Ansted, WV 25812, 304-658-4910.

Rooms: 2, both with private bath. Children welcome. Sorry, no pets or smoking. Check out is 11 a.m.

Rates: $ 65. per night; includes breakfast. Accept Mastercard, Visa, check or cash.

Open: Memorial Day through third weekend in October.

Facilities and activities: Fishing, hiking, and white water rafting at nearby state parks. African American Museum is on the premises.

BEAVER

House of Grandview Bed & Breakfast

Imogene and Gordon Dodd invite you to visit them at the House of Grandview Bed & Breakfast, a modern house cozy enough to call home. There are two bedrooms with private baths and two bedrooms with a shared bath. From April 15 - October 31 guests can rent the "Deer Head Cottage" out back. This small guest house has its own bath, small refrigerator, microwave, and coffee pot.

Also available on the property for the guests' enjoyment are a hot tub in the gazebo, gas grill, hammock, swing, fire ring, horseshoes, volley ball, badminton, and croquet. Guests are invited to make themselves at home in the recreation room, living room and dining room, and on the deck.

House of Grandview is located in Beaver, about eight miles west of

Beckley. The area is well-known for the outdoor drama performed six nights a week from June through August at nearby Grandview State Park. Also nearby are the New River Gorge, scenic overlooks, and four excellent golf courses.

How to get there: From I-64 take the Grandview Exit onto Grandview 9 North. Go 1.2 miles north to the First Southern Baptist Church, turn left onto Old Grandview Road Go 1.1 miles to Jefferson Drive. Go right on Jefferson to the first driveway on your right.

Innkeepers: Imogene and Gordon Dodd

Address/Telephone: 680 Grandview Road, Beaver, WV 25813, 304-763-4381/800-850-6479, fax 304-763-3358.

Rooms: 2 with private bath, 2 with shared bath; 1 cabin with private bath. Sorry, no pets; call about children. Smoking in designated areas only; no smoking in bedrooms. Check out is 11 a.m.

Rates: $ 55. - 75. per night double occupancy; includes full breakfast. Cash and checks accepted.

Open: Year around.

Facilities and activities: Nearby are the New River Gorge, Grandview National Park, and Little Beaver State Park. Outdoor activities such as white water rafting, golf, hiking, biking, paddle boats, and swimming are all available in the area.

FAYETTEVILLE

The County Seat

Driving down Maple Avenue in Fayetteville, you will surely notice the lovely grounds and porches of The County Seat. Built in 1910 by a legendary Fayette County sheriff, your hosts Eddie and Pat Bennett invite you to visit their distinctive home, and stay in one of its four gabled guest rooms. Two of the gabled rooms are double occupancy and have private baths. The other two guest rooms have double beds. These two rooms share a large Victorian bath, featuring an enormous claw foot tub and shower.

Guests will enjoy a silver service breakfast featuring local produce in season, served at the guests' convenience. Breakfast is served in the dining room, or weather permitting, on the verandah. Guests are invited to relax in rockers on the porch, in the library, or in the parlor with its working fireplace.

After relaxing at The County Seat, a short walk will take you to downtown historic Fayetteville. Enjoy restaurants; antique, book, and coffee shops; or inquire at the local outfitters about exciting white water trips.

How to get there: From I-64/I-77 take Exit 48 and head north on U.S. 19. Turn right at the Laurel Creek Road exit, then left onto Maple Avenue. House with sign is 1/8 mile on the left.

Innkeepers: Eddie and Pat Bennett

Address/Telephone: 306 West Maple Avenue, Fayetteville, WV 25840, 304-574-0823.

Rooms: 4, 2 with private baths. Children welcome; sorry, no pets or smoking.

Rates: $ 75. private bath; $ 65. shared bath; includes breakfast. Credit cards not accepted.

Open: April through early November.

Facilities and activities: Nearby are the New River Gorge National River Visitors Center, and New River Gorge Bridge. Fayetteville offers shopping and restaurants, as well as major outdoor recreation outfitters to assist you in athletic explorations of the area.

Cozy Cottage Bed & Breakfast

Cozy Cottage Bed & Breakfast is located in Fayetteville on two beautiful acres of the historic McIntosh-McCaleb House, the latter being circa 1893. Your innkeepers, Ken and Lita Eskew, reside in the main house and rent the cottage which lies on the rear of the property.

The cottage, an adorable white clapboard house, offers home style hospitality in a private atmosphere. Views from the cottage are of the lovely grounds and Lita's flourishing gardens. The cottage consists of a living room, bedroom, full bath, and full kitchen. The living room sofa pulls out to sleep two, and there is a double bed in the bedroom. The cottage is perfect for a family or two couples wanting their own quarters. The cottage has central air and television. Guests are invited to help themselves to the continental breakfast which is provided in their own kitchen, and to prepare other meals as they wish. This is a charming and comfortable spot. There is a 72-hour cancellation policy.

How to get there: Take Route 19 to Fayetteville. From Court Street, turn right onto West Maple at stoplight. Travel down West Maple for approximately .5 mile; look for white bungalow style house with small sign out front.

Innkeepers: Ken & Lita Eskew

Address/Telephone: 302 West Maple Avenue, Fayetteville, WV 25840, 304-574-0134.

Rooms: Cottage rented as one unit, sleeps up to 4. Sorry, no pets, smoking, or children under 10. Check out is 10 a.m.

Rates: $ 75. per night double occupancy; $ 15. for each additional person. Includes continental breakfast. Accept cash or personal check.

Open: Year around.

Facilities and activities: An ever growing area for white water rafting and other outdoor sports, visitors will be pleased to discover the numerous rafting and rock climbing outfitters, bicycle shops, and restaurants in the nearby downtown area.

Morris Harvey House Bed and Breakfast

The Morris Harvey House was built in 1902 and is on the National Register of Historic Places. The house is a Queen Anne-style Victorian with 14 rooms, lovely gardens, a wraparound porch, and a wrought iron gate surrounding the grounds. The house was built for the prominent lawyer Morris Harvey by R. H. Dickinson. The architect was George Barber. Morris Harvey was a Confederate veteran, famous banker and churchman, and served as sheriff of Fayette County from 1859-61, and 1865-69. Harvey was also president of the Continental Divide Gold and Silver Company. He is best remembered for his generous contributions to the establishment of Morris

Harvey College in Charleston, West Virginia, now part of The University of Charleston.

There are four guest rooms to rent, each having a private bath. The Rosa Suite is a romantic retreat for special occasions and features an antique brass bed. Its connecting full bath has an antique shower, and brass footed tub. The Grand Suite has a full bay window that contains an antique day bed enclosed with fretwork and stained glass. Furnishings include a queen size "cannonball" bed, fireplace, and full bath. This room can accommodate three people. The Harvey Room has a full size antique bed and an adjoining half bath. Its full antique bath is just down the hall. The Loft is a secluded area on the third floor featuring a full antique brass bed, sitting room, and full bath. Of the guest rooms, the Rosa Suite and the Loft both have air-conditioning, although with the cool summers in Fayetteville, one rarely needs it!

How to get there: Take Route 19 South from Summersville, or Route 19 North from Beckley to the Fayetteville Historic District exit. Enter on Court Street; take right on Court Street to 201 West Maple.

Innkeeper: Elizabeth Bush

Address/Telephone: 201 West Maple Avenue, Fayetteville, WV 25840, 304-574-1902, fax 304-574-1040.

Web page: http://bbchannel.com/bbc/p205972.asp

Rooms: 4, each with private bath. Children and pets welcome; sorry, no smoking. Check out 11 a.m., 10 a.m. on Sundays.

Rates: $ 85. per night includes breakfast. Visa, Mastercard, traveler's checks, cash accepted.

Open: April 1 - November 1.

Facilities and activities: White water rafting, rock climbing,, rappelling, biking, canoeing, and hiking. Within walking distance of shops and restaurants in historic downtown Fayetteville. Located near the New River Gorge Bridge, Babcock State Park, Hawk's Nest State Park, and Beckley Exhibition Coal Mine.

White Horse Bed & Breakfast

It's quite possible that your first greeting at the White Horse Bed & Breakfast will come from Snickers and Mars, the owners' adorable schnauzer and schnauzer/border collie. If you don't care for dogs, these two are so small and sweet you'll find them no trouble. However, they may win you over yet, as their owner gives testimony to the many cards and letters arriving from guests who have grown attached to Snickers and Mars.

The dogs were the second pleasant surprise upon my arrival, my first being the view of the house and its lovely grounds. The third was my warm welcome from owner and proprietor Jane Vosler. As she climbed down from a ladder where she was meticulously tending to some beautiful woodwork, I quickly realized she is a dynamo and gets a lot done. Good thing, as she described the poor condition of the house when she and her husband bought it over a decade ago. Today the house is amazing.

The 22 room mansion, sitting on 28 acres, was built in 1906 by Fayette County Sheriff E.B. Hawings. The important architecture and meticulous preservation of the house by the Voslers' have earned it a listing on the National Register of Historic Places. I think my favorite physical feature of the house are its dining room murals. The murals were hand painted by a well-known artist of the time, Zuber, and were shipped to Fayetteville from Paris. Sources in New York say the pattern, "El Dorado," is still available, and that the murals' current replacement cost would be around $ 60,000. Enjoy your delicious breakfast, complete with china and silver, while you take in the magnificence of these murals.

The house itself is 10,000 square feet. There are six bedrooms to rent, each named after a river in West Virginia: the New, Gauley, Meadow, Kanawha, Greenbrier, and the Cheat. All the rooms are lovely, and feature queen, double or twin beds. Some have private baths and some shared baths.

Guests are invited to relax in the cheerful sun room, the library complete with liqueur cabinet, or the lovely living room. Also for rent is the quaint cottage in the rear. It has a living room with a queen size sleep sofa, a bedroom with king size bed, private bath, and full kitchen. The cottage is perfect for families or a group of white water rafters. Reservations are recommended, especially on weekends. The Voslers' hospitality guarantees that they have many repeat visitors, including the Ambassador of Mexico. A haven for writers, the B & B has been featured in *Southern Living* magazine, as well as newspapers from Austin to Boston.

If you just can't tear yourself away from the White Horse, you may not have to. The Voslers have completed the construction of a road to an exclusive set of lots which are for sale for private homes. Rest assured that the Voslers have seen to it that distinct covenants preside over the development, guaranteeing that the privacy and beauty of White Horse goes on uninterrupted.

How to get there: From I-77/I-64, take the North Beckley exit and head north on U.S. 19 to Fayetteville. Go past the courthouse and through two stoplights; take next left onto Fayette Avenue. House is on the right with large visible sign.

Innkeepers: Cleon and Jane Vosler

Address/Telephone: 120 Fayette Avenue, Fayetteville, WV 25840, 304-574-1400.

Web page: wvweb.com/www/white_horse_bb/

Rooms: 6 in main house; 3 with private bath; cottage for rent in back. Small pets and children welcome; smoking permitted in library.

Rates: $ 85. shared bath; $ 95. private bath; $ 110. cottage; $ 150. for 4 in the suite. Includes full breakfast. Cash or personal check only. Military, travel agent, and 3-day stays receive 10% discount.

Open: Year around.

Facilities and activities: New River Gorge National Park, white water rafting, hiking, skiing, golfing, fishing, hunting, and kayaking. To relax from all these outdoor activities, visit restaurants, craft and antique shops, area malls and theaters.

Wisteria House Bed & Breakfast

Innkeepers Denise and Matt Scalph offer one of the more unique bed and breakfast arrangements I have come across. Matt runs a full old-fashioned barber shop in part of the house. He offers a straight razor shave with hot towels and usually has customers waiting in line, sharing local gossip. Denise recently opened a gift shop in the lower part of the house, featuring West Virginia products, one-of-a-kind crafts, and gift baskets. A trip to Wisteria House could find you clean shaven and with all your shopping done!

The Scalphs opened the bed & breakfast in 1996, naming it after the abundant wild wisteria covering the rear of the property, and visible from the comfortable back porch. The original part of the house is dated from around 1930. While visiting, enjoy Denise's full breakfast and gourmet coffee, and save room for her afternoon refreshments, usually accompanied by a freshly baked pie or cake. Guests also have their own coffee set up in their room if they like to enjoy a cup in private. The common sitting rooms feature a VCR and games for adults and children. The three guest rooms for rent are The Baby's Breath, The Magnolia, and The Wisteria Room. All are lovely and spacious. The Wisteria Room has a queen bed with a day bed for a third person. The guest rooms share a very large common bathroom.

There's lots do in and around Fayetteville. The Wisteria House is within walking distance of the downtown theater and restaurants, and five minutes from the Bridgehaven Golf Course. Denise and Matt will make you feel at home at The Wisteria House.

How to get there: From I-65/I-77 take North Beckley exit. Travel north on U.S. 19 through Fayetteville. After courthouse and second light, house is on left.

Innkeepers: Denise and Matt Scalph

Address/Telephone: 147 South Court Street, Fayetteville, WV 25840, 304-574-3678.

Rooms: 3, with shared bath. Sorry, no pets, smoking, or children under 12. Check out 10 a.m.

Rates: $ 75. per night with full breakfast. Visa, Mastercard, personal check, or cash.

Open: Year around.

Facilities and activities: Sightseeing, rafting, mountain biking, hiking and rock climbing. Within walking distance of shopping, restaurants and theater.

GHENT

Farmhouse in Green Pastures

Basil and BeeBee Shrewsberry invite you to rent their 100-year old farmhouse in Ghent, West Virginia. Close to golf courses, white water rafting, state parks, and skiing, the Farmhouse in Green Pastures is convenient whatever your interest.

The two-story farmhouse has been refurbished, and has 3 bedrooms which can sleep 10 to 13 guests. The house has two baths and a full kitchen. In winter, guests enjoy sitting around the wood stove and drinking hot chocolate while they re-live their skiing exploits – the Farmhouse is only 5 minutes from the slopes at Winterplace. In summer, visitors enjoy the swing and rockers on the front porch. Guests can have their hosts plan a hay ride and wiener roast. For a touch of nostalgia, draw water from the old well at the rock cellar, or even visit the nice outhouse.

The property has forest trails and pasture land for pleasant hikes; some guests enjoy helping Basil feed the cattle. When the snow flies your hosts have plenty of sleds and hills for sledding. As if all this weren't enough, the Farmhouse is near four state parks, the craft center Tamarack in Beckley, and numerous other attractions. Plan a trip to the Farmhouse – where the outdoor tranquility eases the most harried guest.

How to get there: From I-77 take Exit 28 to Ghent. Next take Route 48 West (Odd Road) 1.5 miles from exit.

Innkeepers: Basil and BeeBee Shrewsberry

Address/Telephone: P. O. Box 177, Ghent, WV 25843, 304-787-5722/ 304-787-3009.

Rooms: 3 bedroom farmhouse with 2 baths and kitchen. Children and pets welcome; large pets require deposit. Sorry, no smoking or alcoholic beverages.

Rates: Summer: $ 80. double occupancy; $ 120. for 4 persons; add $ 20. per additional guest. Winter: $ 140. for up to four persons; add $ 20. per additional. Includes continental breakfast. Accept cash and check.

Open: Year around.

Facilities and activities: Nearby are outdoor drama at Grandview, four state parks, three golf courses, white water rafting, skiing, and the Beckley Exhibition Coal Mine.

LANSING

Mill Creek Luxury Cabins

Enjoy the atmosphere of beautiful West Virginia mountains in the heart of the New River Gorge. Visitors to Mill Creek Luxury Cabins will enjoy sitting on the decks watching gorgeous sunsets or taking a relaxing soak in the outdoor hot tubs, all in a tranquil wooded setting. Each of the seven luxury cabins is decorated in its own signature style. Different cabins feature stained glass, original art, and wonderful design features. Several of the cabins have been decorated in a southwestern style. The cabins are all owner designed and built – which gives you an idea of how talented your hosts are.

Six of the cabins are equipped to accommodate eight people. Each cabin has a complete kitchen, bath, dining and living area. They also have two full bedrooms downstairs with queen size beds, and two queen size beds upstairs in the loft. Each cabin also has a wood burning fireplace and a hot tub on the deck. The large cabin has all these amenities, plus more. This cabin has satellite television, air conditioning, washer and dryer, and a meeting room. The large cabin sleeps 14 persons.

How to get there: Mill Creek Cabins are located .5 mile from the interchange of Route 19 on Milroy Grose Road, 1.5 miles north of the New River Gorge Bridge and the Canyon Rim Visitors Center of New River Gorge National Park.

Innkeepers: Revonna and Neil Redman

Address/Telephone: P. O. Box 148, Lansing, WV 25862, 304-658-5005/ 800-692-5005.

Web page: www.millcreekcabins.com

E-mail: revonna@millcreekcabins.com

Rooms: 6 cabins sleeping 8; 1 cabin sleeping 14. Children welcome; sorry, no pets. Smoking permitted.

Rates: Cabins $ 120. per night double occupancy with $ 20. per additional person; large cabin $ 200. per night double occupancy with $ 20. per additional person. Accept Visa, Mastercard, cash and check.

Open: Year around.

Facilities and activities: Open fields for frisbee, volleyball and horseshoes; charcoal grill and outside fire pit; hot tubs and wood burning fireplaces in each cabin; towels and linens provided. Area attractions: rafting, horse back riding, golf, hiking, hunting, fishing, biking, rock climbing, skiing and skydiving.

LEWISBURG

Lynn's Inn Bed & Breakfast

Driving to Lynn's Inn Bed & Breakfast, just a quick jaunt down Route 219 from downtown Lewisburg, you quickly reach the green rolling hills and mountain ridges that make the Inn's setting so spectacular. Lynn's Inn is set on substantial acreage, which has been in the McLaughlin family for many years. The Inn is currently owned and operated by Lynn and Richard McLaughlin. Years ago there were only three places to stay along Route 219. Back when they were called "tourist homes", they offered a night's lodging, but no breakfast. The "McLaughlin Tourist Home" was among them, and was operated by Richard's parents for thirty years. Lynn reopened the house in 1990 as Lynn's Inn Bed & Breakfast, but retained its old-time hospitality.

Once you enter the inn, the first thing you are likely to see, or hear, is Scarlett, a beautiful blue and red parrot. I had never seen a bird with this coloring. If it's cold out guests will quickly notice the cozy wood stove. Usually booked on weekends, Lynn's Inn stays busy mainly with referrals and repeat customers. Their busiest season corresponds with the area's nicest weather, April through November. Lynn's husband still operates the property as a small beef cattle farm. If you're a big breakfast eater, you'll enjoy fresh eggs on your visit, along with the rest of Lynn's bountiful country breakfast, with two meats, hash brown potato cakes, and homemade breads. Guests enjoy looking at the horse and pygmy goats, who love to be petted, as well as the many chickens and ducks.

Guests are encouraged to use the downstairs living room or upstairs sitting room for relaxing and reading. A refrigerator upstairs is available for guests to use, and is stocked with soft drinks and cold spring water. Each of the four guest rooms have beautiful antique beds. The handmade quilts on the beds were made in Lewisburg.

How to get there: Route 219 north, 3 miles from the town of Lewisburg. Take Exit 169 off I-64, then travel north on 219 for 1.6 miles. The Inn is on the left.

Innkeepers: Lynn & Richard McLaughlin

Address/Telephone: Route 4, Box 40, Lewisburg, WV 24901, 304-645-2003/800-304-2003.

Rooms: 4, all with private bath. Sorry, no smoking, pets or children under 12. Check out is 10 a.m.

Rates. $ 60. - 75.; includes full breakfast. Accept Mastercard and Visa.

Open: All year.

Facilities and activities: Besides all the beauty and adventure available on the nearby Greenbrier River Trail, Lewisburg is the perfect town for antique and window shopping, or getting fresh bread and coffee. The state fair takes place in Lewisburg in August, so plan ahead if you want to visit at that time. The Dandelion Festival is held in May, and the Taste of Lewisburg is held in October, with food vendors along the streets.

The General Lewis Inn

What can I say about the General Lewis? It is one of the most charming inns in the state. Everyone I've met who has stayed here enjoyed it. If you're a history or antique buff . . . .If you like good Southern cooking . . . If you'd like to sit in front of a fire and play chess or read a book . . . If you'd like to play croquet on a green lawn next to the fish pond . . . come to the General Lewis.

The eastern end of the building was built as a residence in the early 1800s by John H. Withrow. It was purchased from Withrow's daughter by Mr. and Mrs. Randolph Hock. It has been operated as an Inn by the Hock family since 1929. The family has spent many years gathering antiques from Greenbrier County and adjoining counties to furnish the Inn. Guests will find spool and canopy beds, old china and glass, old prints and tools, and other delightful antiques throughout the Inn, as well as furnishing each guest room. There are fireplaces in every guest room, each with a charming carved mantel. Wide plank pine floors, vintage and vintage looking fabrics, interesting rugs, chairs, clocks, and photographs guarantee something is always catching your eye. Just thinking about the cozy common area with its comfortable sofa and chairs in front of the fireplace makes me want to visit the Inn again.

Hopefully while at the Inn you'll meet the lovely and charming manager, Nan Morgan. She usually works seven days a week, so you can probably find her. Nan was called back from Colorado several years ago to assist her parents in running the Inn. The General Lewis is busiest from June to October, when it is almost always full on weekends. A full restaurant is open for all three meals every day, for guests and locals. A visit to the General Lewis is always a memorable and charming experience.

How to get there: I-64 to Lewisburg exit, take Route 219 into Lewisburg, turn east on Route 60; the Inn is three blocks from the intersection of Routes 60 and 219, on the right.

Innkeepers: Mary Noel & Jim Morgan, Nan Morgan

Address/Telephone: 301 East Washington Street, Lewisburg, WV 24901, 304-645-2600/800-628-4454, fax 304-645-2600.

Web page: www.virtualcities.com/ons/wv/s/wvsB601.htm

E-mail: nan@generallewisinn.com

Rooms: 120, all with private bath. Children welcome; call about pets. Sorry, no smoking. Check out time 11:00 a.m.

Rates. $ 75. - 125. per night. Winter packages are available. Breakfast, lunch, and dinner served daily in the dining room for additional charge. Additional fee for pets, cribs, or additional guests. Accept major credit cards.

Open: All year.

Facilities and activities: The Inn has a full restaurant, front porch with rockers, croquet behind the Inn with gardens, fish pond and play house. In the area is the Greenbrier River Trail for hiking, biking, and horseback riding. Located in or near Lewisburg are summer theater, shopping, the cultural center Carnegie Hall, and local caves, boating, fishing, skiing and golf.

Swift Level

This beautiful historic mansion lies outside of Lewisburg on 150 acres. The farm, with its original 6,000 acres, was purchased in the 1820s by the great-grandparents of the inn's proprietor, Tootie Jones O'Flaherty.

Swift Level has a two night minimum stay on weekends. Guests may find that at times it takes several months to get a reservation. Two guest rooms are available in the main house, one on the first floor and one on the second, each with a private bath. The downstairs guest room has a unique queen size bed, with a headboard that is like a cupboard. The room itself is elegantly decorated with fine linens and fabrics in shades of mocha, cream, and ivory. Guests staying in this room have the option of eating breakfast in the main dining room, or having breakfast on the private terrace. The upstairs room is just as lovely, with an incredible view of the valley from an upstairs balcony. Likewise, guests in this room may have breakfast in the dining room or be served privately on the balcony.

Also for rent are the Bunkhouse and the Log Cabin. The Bunkhouse lies near the house, and is set up to be rented by one or two families. It contains two bedrooms, each sleeping three guests in handsome custom bunk beds. There are also two bathrooms, and one shared common living area between the two bedrooms. The living area has a working stone fireplace. Guests may also rent the Log Cabin, which lies across a horse pasture from the house. The Cabin is designed to be rented to one family or a group of six or less. The cabin has a full kitchen, but guests can choose to have breakfast at the main house for an additional $ 20. per person. Deposits are required to hold reservations. Reservations canceled with 3 weeks or more notice are completely refundable.

In addition to operating as a luxurious B & B, Swift Level is a working horse farm. It also specializes in equestrian mountain trips, and most of the guests come for that experience. These trips are designed to accommodate the riders' needs and ability. However, riders are encouraged to have substantial experience and conditioning due to the length of the daily rides, and to ensure the comfort of guests. Because of the owner's expertise, the beautiful setting, and the beautiful horses, Swift Level has hosted guests from all over the world, including Singapore, New Zealand, Italy, and France. Tootie also takes riders on rides all over the globe. She has bred horses for over 22 years; her family have been horse lovers and breeders for generations. The horses on the farm currently are all thoroughbreds, quarter horses and imported Irish horses. The ponies are imported Connemara from Ireland. They also have ponies which are a cross of the farm's Connemara and their thoroughbreds.

How to get there: From I-64 at Lewisburg exit, turn left onto Route 219 South, then right on Route 60 West. Go 3 miles, then left on Bunger's Mill Road (also sign for covered bridge); take left on Hern's Mill Road and through gatepost to house. (House and outbuildings are visible from Route 60.)

Innkeepers: Tootie Jones O'Flaherty

Address/Telephone: Route 2, Box 269A, Lewisburg, WV 24901, 304-645-1155, fax 304-647-5212.

Web page: wvweb.com/www/swift_level/

E-mail: swiftlevel@inetone.net

Rooms: 2 in main house, each with private bath; 2 guest houses also available for rent, which sleep between 4 and 6. Children welcome; sorry, no pets. Full gourmet breakfast served daily. Sorry, no TV or smoking. One phone available for all guests.

Rates: $ 80. - 175. per night; includes full breakfast, except for Log Cabin guests. Accept major credit cards.

Open: April through November.

Facilities and activities: Office with fax, telephone and computer available for business travelers. Baby sitting services and massage available with advance notice. Especially noted for Equestrian Mountain Trips, or "Riders' Rides" – for experienced riders only. Lessons available for children and beginners. Available in the area: mountain biking, white water rafting, hiking, canoeing, caving, and skiing. Sightseeing and shopping in nearby historic Lewisburg.

PENCE SPRINGS

Pence Springs Hotel

Originally known as "The Grand Hotel", Pence Springs Hotel has been a premiere retreat because of its historic springs from 1897 until the Great Depression. From 1947 until 1983 Pence Springs served as the State Prison for Women. Current owner Ashby Berkley, whose mother worked at the prison when he was a child, purchased the property in 1986 and launched a million dollar renovation and restoration, returning the hotel to its former elegance. Berkley's extensive restoration of the property has made Pence Springs Hotel a popular resort, attracting visitors from all over. It has been featured in such publications as *Southern Living* and *Gourmet* magazines.

The famous mineral springs around which this resort was founded historically attracted animals and Native Americans to drink from its waters. The Indians followed the indelible bison and buffalo trails to the springs; today horseback riding trails follow the tracks of the long-departed buffalo. In 1872 Andrew Pence acquired the property. After observing all the animals drinking at the springs, he attached a spigot and began bottling and selling the water. Pence Mineral Water won an award at the 1904 World's Fair in St. Louis. Pence built the hotel on the property in 1897. The hotel burned to the ground in 1912. The Grand Hotel was re-built on the site in 1917.

All guest rooms at Pence Springs have a private bath, and include a full breakfast. Rooms are furnished in the style of the 1920s, and suites are also available. Guests will be sure to enjoy the two restaurants on the premises, The Riverside Room and the Sun Porch Café. Two of the most popular features of a stay at the hotel are its Sunday flea markets, which attract more than 135,000 people a year; and the Sunday brunch, served Memorial Day through October.

How to get there: From the south: take I-64 take Exit 161 at Alta; take Route 12 south to Alderson. At Alderson, take Route 12/3 for eight miles further south to Pence Springs. From the north: take I-64 to Exit 139 at Sandstone; follow Route 20 south through Hinton. Next take Route 3 East through Talcott to Pence Springs.

Innkeepers: O. Ashby Berkley & Rosa Lee Berkley Miller

Address/Telephone: P.O. Box 90, Pence Springs, WV 24962, 304-445-2606/800-826-1829, fax 304-445-2204.

Web page: http://wvweb.com/www/Pence_Springs_Hotel

Rooms: 11 rooms and 4 suites. Children and pets welcome; $ 15. surcharge for pets. Smoking allowed in designated areas only.

Rates: $ 60. single rooms - $ 100. for suites; all have private bath. Room rental includes full breakfast; lunch available by reservation. Accept Visa, Mastercard, American Express, Diners Club, Discover, cash or check.

Open: April 1 - December 31. Will open for parties of 25 or more during winter months.

Facilities and activities: Available on grounds are hiking, biking, croquet, horseshoes, fishing on the Greenbrier River, and the popular Sunday flea market. Available nearby are golf, caving, and white water rafting. Travel to historic Lewisburg for restaurants and antique shopping; visit Beckley for the Exhibition Coal Mine and Tamarack, West Virginia's craft showplace.

SANDSTONE

Richmond's Rustic Almost Heaven

The view from the log homes of "Almost Heaven" is so spectacular, that your host William Richmond says "Whether you're staying with us or not, it's worth the drive just for the view." Richmond's Rustic Almost Heaven offers guests the choice of three furnished log homes and a cabin, all located on 30 acres of woodland and open fields on a 200 foot cliff overlooking Sandstone Falls. The perfect place for "getting away from it all."

William Richmond built his log homes using timber from the woods behind the houses, and pulling down the trees using his team of oxen. As you may have gathered by now, Mr. Richmond is a unique and talented individual. He is a fifth generation descendant of the original William Richmond who first settled the area in the late 1700s.

The current 30 acres is part of an original 5,000 acres acquired by the family centuries ago. The nearby town of Sandstone and the Sandstone Falls were originally called New Richmond and Richmond Falls, respectively.

"Almost Heaven" is 1,700 square feet, has three bedrooms, two of which are balcony bedrooms, a large living room, dining room, kitchen and bath. "Riverridge Red" is 2,400 square feet, has 3 bedrooms, 2 baths, a living room, dining room, kitchen, family room and game room. "Poplar Point" is 1200 square feet, has two bedrooms, and is surrounded by the forest for privacy. Each log house has a working fireplace with a coal and wood burning insert. Everything is furnished including linens, towels, pots and pans, and coffee pot; guests need only bring food and personal items. Some basic foodstuffs are also supplied.

This wonderful getaway is located on the New River, and near the Bluestone and Greenbrier Rivers. All three serve as a playground for fishermen, swimmers, and boaters. The surrounding area is also perfect for rafting, hiking, and mountain biking. Some guests prefer to stay on the grounds and spot local wildlife.

How to get there: From I-64 take Exit 139; from I-77 take Exit 14. Take State Route 20 to Hinton. Travel 8 miles down River Road, take the first road on the left past Sandstone Falls Park.

Owner: William Henry Richmond

Innkeeper: Judith K. Bragg

Address/Telephone: P. O. Box 2, Sandstone, WV 25985, 304-466-0874.

Rooms: 3 furnished log homes and one cabin. Children and pets are welcome. Smoking permitted.

Rates: Each log house is $ 60. per night; $ 300. per week. The cottage is $ 50. per night; $ 250. per week. Continental breakfast available upon request. Accept cash or check only.

Open: April 1 through Thanksgiving week.

Facilities and activities: Nearby are outdoor sports on the New, Bluestone, and Greenbrier Rivers, as well as hiking, biking, or horseback riding on the Greenbrier River Trail. Downhill and cross country skiing are available nearby in season.

SUMMERSVILLE

Historic Brock House Bed & Breakfast

Join the many travelers who have visited Brock House for over 100 years. Daniel and Melvina Brock built this Queen Anne farmhouse around the turn-of-the-century to provide lodging for guests when the Nicholas County Court was in session. The tradition of southern hospitality continues in this six guest room bed and breakfast. Guests can choose from spacious rooms with queen or twin beds, private or shared baths, or a two bedroom suite.

Guests will wake to the smell of freshly brewed coffee and home-made breads baking. Guests enjoy breakfast in either the breakfast room or the dining room. Breakfast is served until 9 a.m. Dinner reservations may be made for an additional charge and with sufficient notice. Visitors to Brock House in the warmer months usually enjoy the rockers and wicker furniture on the wraparound porch. During cooler months they are often found around the cozy fireplace visiting with friends or playing cards.

If you care to leave the peace of Brock House, the area offers the best white water rafting in the East, and plenty of outfitting companies to tend to your needs. There are numerous other outdoor activities available, including hiking, biking, rock climbing, and kayaking. Also in the area are antique shops and Civil War battlefields.

How to get there: From I-79 or I-77, take U.S. Route 19. Located on State Route 41 in Summersville.

Innkeeper: Carol & Jim Taylor

Address/Telephone: 1400 Webster Road, Summersville, WV 26651, 304-872-4887, fax 304-872-4887.

Web page: http://bbchannel.com/bbc/p206046.asp

Rooms: 5, 4 with private bath, 1 with shared bath. Sorry, no smoking or pets. Children welcome during the week. Check out 11 a.m.

Rates: $ 70. - 90. double occupancy; includes full breakfast. Accept Visa, Mastercard, cash or personal check.

Open: February through December 23.

Facilities and activities: The area offers white water rafting, rock climbing, Summersville Lake, festivals, kayaking, biking and hiking trails.

WHITE SULPHUR SPRINGS

The James Wylie House Bed & Breakfast

Plan a visit to the quaint town of White Sulphur Springs, and stay at historic James Wylie House. While staying here, take some time to relax in the rockers on the front porch, admiring the gardens of Clifford Parrish and Anne Carberry. Your hosts left the West Coast, seeking a move to the mid-Atlantic to start a B & B. They soon found this charming and historic property, and await making your next stay rewarding.

In the main house are four different, and wonderfully decorated, guest rooms, as well as a two bedroom suite. Breakfast is served in the large formal dining room. In the back of the house is a charming historic log cabin which serves as a guest house. The log cabin can sleep five persons.

Guests interested in outdoor activities can find superb golf, hiking, fishing, mountain biking and skiing all within a very close radius to the James Wylie House. Ask your hosts for information on the Greenbrier River Trail and nearby state parks.

How to get there: I-64 westbound, take exit 18, travel Route 60 west for .9 mile, house is located on the right on Castle Drive; I-64 eastbound, take Exit 175, travel Route 60 east for approximately 4 miles; house is located on the left on Castle Drive.

Innkeepers: Clifford Parrish and Anne Carberry

Address/Telephone: 208 East Main Street, White Sulphur Springs, WV 24986, 304-536-9444/800-870-1613.

Web page: www.travelguides.com/home/james_wylie

E-mail: annec97757@aol.com

Rooms: 4 rooms plus a 2 bedroom suite, all with private baths; also a log cabin guest house which sleeps 5. Children under 6 and certain pet owners encouraged to rent log cabin guest house. Check out 11 a.m.

Rates: $ 65. - 120. for rooms in main house; $ 120 - 140. for cabin.

Gourmet breakfast served daily. Accept Mastercard, Visa, and American Express.

Open: All year.

Facilities and activities: Visit nearby historic Lewisburg for shopping and restaurants. Also located in White Sulphur Springs is the well-known Greenbrier Resort, available for golf, dining and shopping. In the area are several state parks and ski resorts.

WINONA

Garvey House

Explore the gardens, gazebo, and stone walkways on your visit to Garvey House in Winona, West Virginia. The house was built in 1916 by Martin L. Garvey, who served as the superintendent of the Maryland-New River Coal Company. At the time the house was built, Winona was a thriving coal mining town. A distinctive feature of the house is the wide stone wall surrounding the property. The wall was reportedly built by local coal miners.

Guests have the option of renting one of four rooms in the main house, or renting a five bedroom guest house also on the property. Each night's stay in the main house includes a full breakfast. Guests have the option of private or shared baths. There is a wood-fired sauna in the main house in the former root cellar. Lodging in the guest house does not include breakfast, but there is a fully equipped kitchen for guests' use.

Guests especially enjoy exploring the grounds of Garvey House, which feature goldfish ponds, a gazebo, gardens, and stone walkways, all enclosed by the striking stone wall. Upon leaving the property, guests often visit Fayetteville for shopping, eating, or white water rafting, or nearby Beauty Mountain and the New River Gorge for hiking and biking.

How to get there: From the east take I-64 to exit 156 (Sam Black Church). Travel 31 miles west on Route 60 to Lansing Road. Turn left and travel 2 miles on Lansing. At 2 miles you will see a sign that points to the gravel drive; it is only 1/8 mile to Garvey House.

Innkeepers: Chris Terrafranca and Darrell Riedesel

Address/Telephone: 100 Main Street, Winona, WV 25942, 304-574-3235/800-767-3235.

E-mail: garveyhs@cwv.net

Web page: www.visitwv.com/garveyhouse

Rooms: 4 in main house, 3 having shared bath; one 5 bedroom guest house. Children welcome. Smoking permitted outside only.

Rates: $ 54. - 66. per room with full breakfast. $ 225. per night for entire guest house; breakfast not included. Accept cash, check, Mastercard, Visa.

Open: April 1 - October 20.

Facilities and activities: Close to the New River and Gauley River for white water rafting; nearby Beauty Mountain has scenic overlooks with lovely trails for hiking and biking; Fayetteville offers shopping and dining; nearby are opportunities for swimming, fishing, festivals and visiting historic sites.

MORGANTOWN CORRIDOR

Buckhannon, Clarksburg, Fairmont, Morgantown, Orlando, Weston

About the region . . .

Like much of West Virginia, the Morgantown Corridor is a blend of bustling urban areas and picturesque forests and mountains. The biggest city in the region, **Morgantown**, is home to West Virginia University. WVU was the first university in the state, founded in 1867. The school gained nation-wide attention with its superb 1988 football season, and the enthusiastic spirit prevails on fall Saturdays at Mountaineer Field. Morgantown has all the charming attributes of a college town, including an active downtown with restaurants, bookstores, and gift shops. Morgantown's nearby natural environs include Cheat Lake and Coopers Rock State Park, which are reason enough to explain the many outdoor and bike shops you'll find in Morgantown. These stores can quickly have you outfitted for hiking, mountain biking, or white water rafting in the area.

Thirty miles southwest of Morgantown is the town of **Fairmont**, with nearby Pricketts Fort State Park. At Pricketts Fort, visitors can see historic reenactments, envision Indian attacks, and experience life on the original western Virginia border. The park hosts several weekend festivals during the year, including a spring traditional music festival, summer reenactments, the fall Apple Butter Festival, and in December, the 18th Century Christmas Market.

About 45 miles south of Fairmont is the small community of **Buckhannon**, nestled in the Allegheny foothills. This small town is the home of West Virginia Wesleyan College, with the 1,600 seat Wesley Chapel, the largest church in the state. Being a college town means playing host to parents and other out-of-town visitors; Buckhannon has several lovely bed & breakfasts which do just that. In May, try to check out the city's week-long Strawberry Festival.

For more information on the region, contact the Northern West Virginia Convention and Visitors Bureau, 709 Beechurst Avenue, Morgantown, WV 26505, 1-800-458-7373 or 304-292-5081.

BUCKHANNON

Deer Park Country Inn

Lying four miles east of Buckhannon, West Virginia in an incredible setting is the charming Deer Park Country Inn. You approach Deer Park down a long gravel road. Two distinct buildings can be seen from the drive: the main house and the Lodge. The main house, or Inn, is on the left. It is an 1800s farmhouse, with a 1780 log cabin attached to the front. Inside and out there is a rambling feel to the Inn, where additions have appeared over the years. Inside you'll see beautiful hand-hewn beams in the ceiling of the sitting room, and very wide pine plank floors. The sitting room has inviting places to sit, with a cheery fire to escape the chill of a cool day. Many of the floors are painted, in decorative and traditional colors. Nearby are two small adjoining dining rooms, with several individual tables in each room. The tables are situated cozily; guests can visit with each other or not.

The owners have recently converted two rooms into seating for "The Wild Turkey Tavern." The new restaurant offers fine dining for guests and local visitors; reservations are preferred. The Inn also offers catering for private events. Deer Park has an excellent chef, Dale Hawkins, who was trained at the Pittsburgh Culinary Institute. Before coming to Deer Park, he worked at Walt Disney World and had his own restaurant.

As you walk upstairs, enjoy the feel of the glossy curved banister under your hand. All guest rooms have private baths. The Lewis Suite is a "jewel box" set of rooms decorated in paisley and jewel tones. Its bedroom has a queen size bed and two built-in single sleeping alcoves. There is also an adjoining sitting room. Guests staying in The Upshur Room can overlook the pond below and watch the geese and mallards. The Upshur has a double bed as well as an antique child's bed. Located downstairs in the main house is The Randolph Suite. A magnificent antique bed captures your eye first, and next you're looking out the windows to the owner's beautiful garden. The sitting room is lovely, and there is a daybed for additional sleeping.

About 400 feet and a curved drive away from the Inn lies Deer Park Lodge. Its two story, enormous wraparound porch is reminiscent of the Deep South. Inviting wicker chairs and settees greet you as you climb the steps to the porch. My first inclination was to immediately sit and enjoy the view from the porch. My curiosity quickly got the best of me however, and I soon entered the Lodge. When we entered the living room, one couple had a roaring fire going and were cozily in front of it with some sandwiches they had brought for dinner. Next to the front living room is a full kitchen stocked with juice, soda, beer, coffee, tea, and snacks. Next is another common room with a large sofa and fireplace. There are also strategically placed binoculars, which I used the next morning to admire the tiny goslings following their mommy goose around.

There are 3 bedrooms upstairs. The Pocahontas Room has a king size iron bed and a wood-burning stove for cozy nights. The Webster Room features two antique cannonball beds. The Greenbrier Room has an antique queen size sleigh bed. All three bedrooms have private baths, as well as French doors offering both beautiful views and access to the upstairs porch.

Deer Park is a magnificent setting, and is perfect for weddings and other special events. The grounds include 100 acres of meadows, woodland, gardens, rolling hills and two spring-fed stocked ponds. On the grounds there are more than two miles of walking trails, where guests can glimpse deer, wild turkeys, cotton-tailed rabbits, Canadian geese, and wild mallards. We climbed one of the walking trails and saw one of the most spectacular sunsets we could remember.

How to get there: Take U.S. Route 33 to the Old Route 33 exit. Turn left on County Road 151 (old Route 33) and travel one mile to Heavener Grove Road; turn right. Travel 1.3 miles, past an elementary school, to the green mail box. Turn right.

Innkeepers: Liz & Patrick Haynes

Address/Telephone: P. O. Box 817, Buckhannon, WV 26201, 304-472-8400/800-296-8430, fax 304-472-8430.

Web page: www.deerparkcountryinn.com

E-mail: Deerpark@deerparkcountryinn.com

Rooms: 6, all with private baths. Check out at noon. Children welcome. Sorry, no smoking or pets.

Rates: $ 90. - $ 165. double occupancy, includes breakfast. $25. for breakfast for non-guests. 20% discount on rooms Sunday through Thursday. Corporate rates available. Accept Mastercard, Visa, American Express, Discover, Diners Club, Carte Blanche and cash.

Open: All year.

Facilities and activities: Fine dining, croquet, volleyball, fishing, hiking, and a video library. Depending on the weather, guests can dine on the porches or in the garden. Animal lovers will enjoy meeting the family's pedigreed Cavalier King Spaniel. Deer Park offers generous facilities to accommodate weddings, reunions, business meetings and conferences, and other special events.

A Governor's Inn

To return to the days of Victorian grace and charm, step inside the historic Governor's Inn. This century old red brick mansion was built by the second governor of West Virginia, Daniel D. T. Farnsworth, for his wife and fifteen children. Guests will immediately be warmed by both the flames in the fireplace in the grand foyer, as well as the rich gold and red furnishings in the living room. Lovers of old houses will admire the beautiful woodwork and hand carved newel posts and staircase.

The Inn features six tastefully decorated guest rooms, each with air conditioning, television, period furniture and a full size bed. A cozy terry cloth bathrobe awaits each guest. Guests can enjoy classic films, board games or reading in the living room and parlor downstairs. Guests renting the third floor set of rooms have a small kitchen and their own common room to share.

Your hosts, the Hendersons, like to cater to their guests, especially honeymooners and couples celebrating an anniversary. Rose petals on the pillow, champagne, and gourmet desserts make your celebrations a little more special. All guests will love the candlelit gourmet breakfast served in the formal dining room. (Early birds can request coffee and muffins as early as 5 a.m.) Regular items on the menu include the Governor's French toast, casseroles, seasonal drinks, and a specialty of the house, bread pudding with amaretto sauce. Guests are allowed to invite local friends or family to join them at breakfast at the Inn. Desserts and coffee are offered for those guests having a sweet tooth or wanting a treat. Small luncheons and dinners are available with sufficient notice. The Hendersons have also bought the white house next door to the Inn, and have it set up especially for honeymooners, or other guests wanting a little more privacy.

The most unique thing about the Governor's Inn is Jerry Henderson's formidable store of historical knowledge, as well as the "period activities," many for children, which take place at the Inn. The extent of these is such that the Inn distributes a newsletter, "Miss Lillybelle's Academy for Victorian Women," just to outline the schedule of these special activities. The last thing Jerry guarantees is that each guest gets a hug as they leave. If you don't get yours, just ask!

How to get there: From I-79, take Exit 99. Travel east 12 miles on Route 33. Take the Main Street Exit. Go through four stoplights.

From Main Street you will see the B & B, a red brick Victorian on the left.

Innkeepers: Jerry and Bruce Henderson

Address/Telephone: 76 East Main Street, Buckhannon, WV 26201, 304-472-2516/877-246-8466, fax 304-472-1613.

Web page: www.bbonline.com/wv/governor's

E-mail: henderso@msys.net

Rooms: 6, in main house; 2 suites in property next door. Sorry, no smoking or pets. Children welcome.

Rates: $ 69. - 100. double occupancy in the main house; Celebration Suite and Businessman's Suite in White House is $ 100. double occupancy. Includes gourmet breakfast. Accept Mastercard and Visa.

Open: Year around.

Facilities and activities: On premises: historic re-enactments, tea parties, birthday parties, poetry readings, classes on manners, gardening, quilting and more for children and adults. Off premises: Audra and Holly River State Parks, Blackwater Falls State Park, hiking and biking trails, white water rafting (90 minutes away), skiing, Stonewall Jackson Lake, West Virginia University (1 hour away), West Virginia Wildlife Center, historic tours.

CLARKSBURG

Main Street Bed & Breakfast

A trip to the historic district in Clarksburg will soon find you in front of the Main Street Bed & Breakfast. Formerly known as the Freeman-Stout House, it was built in 1872 and is the fourth oldest house in the county. The owners, Bethlyn and David Cluphf, would like you to consider this your home away from home during your stay. The young energetic owners will impress you as they cater to your needs, while also raising their three little ones.

At breakfast, visitors are treated to Bethlyn's home baked breads and muffins, Dave's decadent French toast, omelets, pancakes and fresh ground coffee. Guests can choose from three bedrooms, all with pillow-top beds. An arched entry invites you into the Teaberry Room, which is decorated in warm tones, has a queen size bed, and a private bath with shower. The light and airy Rose Room also has a queen size bed, and invites guests to relax in the antique claw foot tub. The spacious Master Suite boasts a king size bed as well as a twin bed. The room is joined by a large private bath with shower. Guests are also invited to use the downstairs parlor and dining room for their own small gatherings.

How to get there: From I-79, take Route 50 West to Clarksburg, exit Joyce Street, take left to East Main Street. Take right to 151 East Main Street. From 50 East, exit Joyce Street and take a right to East Main, then go right to 151 East Main Street.

Innkeepers: Bethlyn and David Cluphf

Address/Telephone: 151 East Main Street, Clarksburg, WV 26301, 304-623-1440.

Web page: www.bridgeport-clarksburg.com/mainstreet

Rooms: 3, each with private bath. Children welcome. Sorry, no smoking or pets. Check out at 11 a.m.

Rates: $ 60. - 70.; full breakfast included. Visa, Mastercard, American Express, and Discover cards all accepted.

Open: All year.

Facilities and activities: Historic Clarksburg, Pricketts Fort State Park, Fort New Salem, covered bridges, golfing, and shopping.

FAIRMONT

Acacia House Bed & Breakfast

Visitors to Fairmont will want to stay at Acacia House Bed & Breakfast. Acacia House, owned by George and Kathy Sprowls, is located on Locust Avenue. The B & B gets its name from the surrounding locust trees, the locust being in the *acacia* family. The house was built in 1917 for Mr. T. L. Burchinal, the architect for the Marion County Courthouse. Acacia House is a four-story brown brick home with beautiful oak woodwork and six decorative fireplaces. Guests enter through the glass-enclosed front porch, a great place for a lazy afternoon with tea and a book. Guests are invited to relax in the downstairs sitting room, in front of the wood stove and the television. Two guest rooms, the Rose Room and the Evergreen Room, have private baths and queen size beds. These rooms are $ 50. a night single occupancy and $ 70. double occupancy. The Dogwood Room, with a full bed, shares a bath with the Maple Room, which has twin beds. These rooms are $ 45. single occupancy and $ 60.

double occupancy. All rooms include your choice of a continental or full country breakfast.

In addition to a pleasant stay in a lovely restored home, your hosts at Acacia House have special interests which they would love to share with guests . . . in a formal or informal manner. Kathy Sprowls is an avid collector and antique buff – you'll enjoy seeing some of her collections during your stay. Sometimes she has a few antiques for sale. George Sprowls has traveled quite a bit, and is rather an expert on history and politics, which he is happy to discuss. Individuals interested in contacting Kathy and George about formal discussion groups on these topics are encouraged to do so.

Fairmont and Marion County attractions that guests may want to check out include: Pricketts Fort, Barrackville Covered Bridge, Bunner Ridge Park, High Gate Carriage House, and Valley Falls State Park. The Acacia House is also conveniently located to a 51 mile Rail-to-Trail which opened in 1997.

How to get there: From I-79, take Exit 137, take Route 310 to left on Fairmont Avenue. Next turn right on Locust Avenue, and the house is 1.4 miles on the right.

Innkeepers: George and Kathy Sprowls

Address/Telephone: 158 Locust Avenue, Fairmont, WV 26554, tel/fax 304-367-1000/888-269-9541.

Web page: www./acaciahousewv.com

E-mail: acacia@acaciahousewv.com

Rooms: 4, 2 with private baths, 2 with shared bath. Children welcome; sorry, no smoking or pets. Check out is 11 a.m.

Rates: $ 45.- 70.; includes full breakfast. Mastercard, Visa, Discover, personal check and cash accepted.

Open: All year.

Facilities and activities: Several state parks are located nearby, offering hiking, swimming, fishing, hunting, and canoeing. Also nearby are skiing, antiquing, and numerous fairs and festivals throughout the year.

MORGANTOWN

Almost Heaven Bed & Breakfast

Let gracious Cookie Coombs and her husband make you comfortable at Almost Heaven Bed & Breakfast. Located in a relatively new house, Almost Heaven is beautifully decorated with an attention to detail. Relax in the elaborate Victorian Parlor or the comfortable library, complete with a cozy fireplace and extensive videotape library. In good weather, enjoy the view from the back porch of the beautiful mountains surrounding Morgantown.

Almost Heaven enjoys a steady business of repeat clients, including many state and federal employees. One word of warning – this is "Mountaineer Country," meaning that during WVU football season, rooms are reserved weeks and months in advance. Guests at Almost Heaven will enjoy lots of earthly pleasures. Among them are feather beds and large country breakfasts, including eggs, pork chops, and potatoes, among other things. Bring your appetite.

How to get there: At the intersection of I-68 and I-79, take Exit 1 on I-68 to a stop sign. Go left on Route 119 North to stoplight, turn left on Scott Avenue. Travel one mile to white house on left.

Innkeepers: Cookie and Jim Coombs.

Address/Telephone: 391 Scott Avenue, Morgantown, WV 26505, tel/fax 304-296-4007 or 800-CALL WVA.

Web page: www.sbccom.com/vid/almost heaven

Rooms: 4 rooms, all with private baths; also one suite. Sorry, no smoking, pets or children under 16. Check out 11 a.m.

Rates: $ 75. - 85. per night; suite is $ 150. per night. No discounts, but weekly and monthly rates available; also accept per diems for state employees. Accept all major credit cards.

Open: All year.

Facilities and activities: Hiking on premises, wild turkeys, deer, and a fox can be seen on property. Close to: Scenic Coopers Rock, Forks of Cheat Winery, Cheat Lake, WVU Football Stadium and Coliseum.

Appelwood Bed & Breakfast

Guests coming to Appelwood Bed & Breakfast should look for the unusual mailbox across the street from the driveway. The mailbox is in the shape of a two-story wood shingled house, and has a wooden apple swinging from the box. Appelwood has been open for several years, and is a modern post and beam house. Built in the traditional manner with traditional materials, the house is situated on the second highest peak in Monongalia County, on 35 mostly wooded acres. Located only 4 miles from Morgantown, Appelwood provides a peaceful retreat for busy parents' or football weekends, or just a beautiful stay in the country. You approach Appelwood B & B by driving up a hill on a long gravel drive. The house is surrounded by well-tended grounds, with lovely gardens and stone paths. On my visit a gray kitty was enjoying the sunny stone paths and waiting for a tummy scratch.

A beautiful treasure awaits you when you see the house. The construction of the house is especially interesting, but without knowing much about the technical aspects of the house, anyone simply seeing the house will be struck by its unique features. The facade of the house is constructed of innumerable light-colored stones, which are tightly packed in asymmetrical rows. Most of the stones appear to be smaller and thinner than an average brick. The effect is very striking, and makes one appreciate old world craftsmanship. Next you may notice the enormous hand carved wooden double doors. A quick trip to the side of the house and you'll see that one side of the structure consists almost entirely of glass, broken only by a few beams and a huge stone fireplace. All of the stonework in the house was done by Bob Lewis, a talented stonemason from the Fairmont area. The main house is built primarily of oak and chestnut timbers which are over 100 years old. The timbers on the front wall came from the old home place on the Huff Farm near Mannington. Both the front door and fireplace have iron hardware which was especially designed for the house. After viewing this extraordinary house, you will be amazed to learn that the 40 tons of new oak comprising the main frame of the structure are held together without the use of bolts and screws. This stunning house is not merely an engineering feat, but a treat for the eyes.

The main house has a one bedroom guest suite with bath, kitchen and living room. A separate guest house is appointed with walnut cabinets, and exposed post and beam construction. Both facilities have air conditioning. While the owners can describe the building of almost every nook and cranny to construction buffs, guests like me might enjoy learning about the hot tub and sauna, both of which have room for four people. The sauna area opens onto a full greenhouse. And did I mention the large inviting decks as well as the lovely in-ground pool, both of which looked inviting on an unusually warm day in Monongalia County. There are also a swing and a hammock in the backyard for lazy days. At night or in cool weather guests can enjoy satellite TV in the den. Horse lovers can bring their horses to board on the farm.

How to get there: From I-79 take the Goshen Road exit. Go to the stop sign on old Route 73. Go 1.5 miles, the driveway is on the right.

Innkeepers: Jim Humbertson and Gordon Clizzer

Address/Telephone: Route 5, Box 137, Morgantown, WV, 304-296-2607.

Web page: www.appelwood.com

E-mail: appelwood@aol.com

Rooms: 2, both with queen size beds and private baths. Smoking allowed in designated areas. Call about children and pets. Check out at 11 a.m.

Rates: $ 55. - 75., with weekly rates available. Includes full breakfast. Mastercard, Visa, and cash accepted.

Open: Year around.

Facilities and activities: On the premises are an in-ground pool, hot tub, sauna, and greenhouse, as well as 35 acres to explore. Nearby are West Virginia University, Cheat Lake, Coopers Rock State Park, Forks of Cheat Winery, white water rafting, and skiing.

Chestnut Ridge Commons Bed & Breakfast

Chestnut Ridge Commons Bed & Breakfast is located in scenic Morgantown, between the Evansdale and Downtown campuses of West Virginia University. This former elementary school offers the amenities of a traditional bed & breakfast, along with the conveniences of a fully equipped business center. Built in the early 1900s, Chestnut Ridge School served as a small community-based elementary school until 1978. Morgantown architect Samuel Bonasso and his wife Nancy undertook the restoration of the abandoned school in the late 1980s. Chestnut Ridge and its new addition comprise Chestnut Ridge Commons, which features 6,000 square feet of unique architecture. Many modern changes have been made, but visitors can still see the fifteen foot ceilings, wide oak staircases, ten foot windows, hanging globe lights, and hardwood floors of the original structure.

Guests can choose from 5 sleeping options: The first suite is the "Candle Rose," decorated with the plate quilt pattern. The second suite, called "Tempest in a Teacup," has furnishings which mix floral patterns and stripes . . . the owner suggests relaxing with a cup of tea in this room. The third suite is named "Quilted Dreams." The relaxing blue shades in this room may encourage guests to snuggle under its many cotton quilts. The fourth suite, "Hunterwood," has walls of forest green and a wall canopy of tapestry fabrics. The velvet footstools look just right for putting your feet up. The fifth suite,

"The Executive," has a wing-back recliner for all those serious business plans to be made . . . right after enjoying the luxurious jacuzzi and first class bedding in this suite.

All guests can enjoy a gourmet breakfast, complimentary newspapers, an exercise room, snacks, and the VCR and movie collection. With prior notice, your hosts will arrange for laundry/dry cleaning, errand service, temporary secretary service, or ground transportation. The facility is an excellent site for almost any business meeting or function.

How to get there: Take Exit 7 from I-68, follow signs for Route 119 North, go .75 miles. At the bottom of the hill continue straight on 119 North; at first traffic light turn left on Stewartstown Road. At the next light continue straight on Stewartstown and B & B is 300 yards on right. From I-79, take Exit 155. Go .5 miles and turn right; cross blue bridge, at first light go straight. Go left at next light on to Patterson Drive. Go through first light to Route 705; take Route 705 through two more lights. At third light, turn right; B & B is 300 yards ahead.

Innkeeper: Fonda Holehouse

Address/Telephone: 1000 Stewartstown Road, Morgantown, WV 26505, 304-598-9594.

Web page: http://bbchannel.com/bbc/p206040.asp

Rooms: Four suites each with private bath; luxury suite with meeting room. Check out at 11 a.m.

Rates: Call for rates. Stay includes gourmet breakfast. Mastercard, Visa, American Express, cash or personal check accepted.

Open: Year around.

Facilities and activities: Nearby: Top-notch recreational facilities, fine dining, state parks, NCAA sports, and beautiful mountain scenery. Other local attractions include Cheat Lake, snow skiing at Wisp, the WVU Creative Arts Center, Lakeview and Pineview Golf Courses, local dinner theater, shopping, and seasonal fairs and festivals.

Fieldcrest Manor

Fieldcrest Manor was built around 1920 by Thoney Pietro — a well-known stonemason in Morgantown. You arrive at Fieldcrest by driving up a curvy, hilly, shaded drive. The cozy house is set on a hill with picturesque views of the rolling hills surrounding it. The University's agricultural farm is across the street. Guests at Fieldcrest can enjoy views of the cows and calves in the neighboring fields while they relax on the tiled front terrace. While you sit on the terrace, one of the friendly cats may come up for a rub.

Entering Fieldcrest you'll find an immaculate and inviting bed and breakfast. There are five guest rooms to choose from. The first is the Pompili Room, named after the owner's contractors. It is furnished with dark furniture and has a large bath with both a shower and tub. The next room is the Cedar Room, covered with the original cedar paneling. Interesting antique light fixtures were found by the owners and installed in this guest room. The last guest room on the first floor is the Rose Room. Both the Cedar and Rose rooms have lovely baths with showers. Upstairs are the last two guest rooms, Sarah's Room and the Country Room. Again, both rooms have their own private baths.

Fieldcrest Manor was purchased by Susan and Cliff Linkous when Dr. Linkous retired from his medical practice. Susan Linkous and the innkeeper, Sarah Lough, will fix you a delicious breakfast any time from 6:30 to 9:30, just pick the time. Fieldcrest is situated on five acres, so if you have extra time, explore the grounds. You are likely to stumble upon the grape arbor or blackberry or blueberry bushes. After dark the grounds are especially peaceful, and visitors may enjoy watching the fireflies underneath the trees.

Of course while staying at Fieldcrest, you are in Mountaineer Country, the home of West Virginia University. Local shops and outfitters can assist visitors in finding out about mountain biking, rock climbing and hiking in the region. You'll also be very close to Coopers Rock State Park and Cheat Lake. During football season, make reservations as early as possible.

How to get there: From Interstate 68: take Exit 7, Pierpont Road. Take Route 857 South. Go straight through two lights, picking up Route 119 North. Continue 1.2 miles to next light. Turn left onto

Stewartstown Road, Route 67. Fieldcrest Manor will be .8 mile on your left. From Interstate 79: take Exit 155, Star City. Go .5 mile and turn right toward Morgantown. Go straight through the first light. At the second light, turn right on Route 705. Go through next two lights, at third light, turn left onto Stewartstown Road. Fieldcrest Manor is .8 mile on the right. There is a well-lit sign to mark the driveway.

Owner: Susan Linkous

Innkeeper: Sarah Lough

Address/Telephone: 1440 Stewartstown Road, Morgantown, WV 26505, 304-599-2686/800-765-0569, fax 304-599-2853.

Web page: www.pinnaclemall.com/fieldcrestmanor

E-mail: fldcrest@access.mountain.net

Rooms: 5, all with private bath. Sorry, no smoking or pets. House not child-proof. Check-out 11 a.m.

Rates: $ 75. single occupancy; $ 90. Double; special weekends and holidays $ 100. Includes full breakfast. Accept Mastercard, Visa, check, or cash.

Open: Year around.

Facilities and activities: On premises: five acres for walking and picnicking; bicycles available. Nearby: West Virginia University sporting events and campus, Coopers Rock State Park, Cheat Lake, public theater, winery, boating, hunting, hiking and mountain biking.

ORLANDO

Friendsheep Farm Bed & Breakfast

Friendsheep Farm, located on 230 beautiful acres, is the perfect get away for nature lovers as well as those seeking old-time ambiance. Every effort has been made at Friendsheep Farm to replicate farm life from a hundred years ago – with the addition of a few modern amenities! Guests are invited to bring their own horses to ride and explore the property. Other activities nearby are Jackson's Mill, Historic Bulltown, Stonewall Jackson Lake, and Burnsville Lake. There is a pond for swimming on the property. However, there is no lifeguard, so swimming is at your own risk.

The wood used to build the farmhouse was cut on the farm itself. The property was settled by two Davis brothers — and their families — affluent farmers from northern West Virginia. The Davis family were the early owners of a Delco generator, as well as one of the first refrigerators in the area. People traveled from miles around to see the electric lights and the machine-made ice. One of the brothers made a spectacle driving his car around the area, cars being very uncommon at the time.

Friendsheep Farm offers two different options for guests. Guests can stay in the main house, which is a 100-year old Victorian, and has been lovingly renovated in that period. There are three bedrooms for guests in the main house, which share two baths. Guests staying in the main house are served a full breakfast, which is included with their room. The Farm has "Primestar" satellite television, as well as a cozy gas log fireplace, if you wear yourself out on the hiking trails. The second sleeping option is staying in an outbuilding called the "Cellar House Suite." The suite has a 14' x 24' bedroom, along with its own private bath and kitchen. The suite also has air conditioning, gas logs, and its own deck. For those wanting lots of privacy, the suite is perfect.

How to get there: Take I-79 south of Weston to the Roanoke exit. Exit left onto Route 19 North toward Weston. Go an 1/8 to 1/4 of a mile to Goosepen Road. Take a left and go 12.5 miles on Goosepen Road to the house and outbuildings on your right.

Innkeeper: Diana Gooding

Address/Telephone: Route 1, Box 158, Orlando, West Virginia 26412, 304-462-7075.

Rooms: 3 bedrooms, 2 baths in main house. The Cellar House Suite has a private kitchen and bath. Prefer no children; small pets permitted if healthy and flea-free!

Rates: In main house, $ 65. single, $ 75. double occupancy; breakfast included. Suite is $ 75. single, $ 85. double; breakfast optional. Accept cash or check only.

Open: May 1 - October 31; suite is available at other times with sufficient notice.

Facilities and activities: Hiking trails, camping, fishing, swimming. Guests can bring their own horse for trail riding. Massages available by reservation.

WESTON

Natural Seasons Bed & Breakfast

Natural Seasons Bed & Breakfast is a renovated, turn-of-the-century Federal style home decorated with a seasonal theme. Each of the four bedrooms is lovingly and creatively decorated with the motif of one of the four seasons. Each has a private bath. The Spring and Summer rooms have gas fireplaces. The Fall bedroom includes a whirlpool bathtub. The Winter bedroom is decorated with a pristine white quilt and a beautiful arrangement of stark branches. A full breakfast is included with each night's stay. When guests arrive, they determine when they would like breakfast to be served.

A visit to Natural Seasons Bed & Breakfast will leave you amazed at the energy and ideas of its owners, John and Carol Williams. John is a professor and naturalist, and is the founder and proprietor of the

"Earth Link Company." Earth Link offers educational services and products to engage individuals in learning more about the natural world. Nature Studies are offered by a team of Earth Link naturalists on a weekly basis. These studies and hikes are open to guests and the general public. As you enter the B & B, you'll see on your left a common area complete with a library of books, videotapes, audiocassettes, and computer programs about nature and the environment.

In addition to the library and nature studies available, John can explain many of the energy saving devices in the house. These include all of the Swedish appliances in the spacious, modern kitchen, as well as the water-saving toilets and washing machine. Natural Seasons offers unique opportunities to learn about our environment. For those guests simply wanting to rest and relax, this is a beautiful place to do that, too. The Williams' have plans to add a deck and sauna in the near future, for even more relaxing.

How to get there: From I-79, take Exit 96 to south Weston, turn north on Rt. 19 and continue into town. As the road becomes one-way, look for Natural Seasons on the left in the first block of Center Avenue.

Innkeepers: John and Carol Williams

Address/Telephone: 17 Center Avenue, Weston, WV 26452, 304-269-7902, fax 304-269-7902.

Web page: http://www.wvonline.com/naturallifeways

E-mail: natseas@neumedi.net

Rooms: Four, all with private bath. Full breakfast included. Sorry, no smoking or pets. Well-behaved children welcome with responsible adult.

Rates: $ 65. double occupancy; weekend specials offered frequently. Government employees on business receive 10% discount. Accept Mastercard and Visa.

Open: Year round.

Facilities and activities: Small bookstore and nature study center. Nature studies offered, including hikes and discussions. Glass factory nearby in Jane Lew; antique and craft shopping in historic Weston.

THE COAL FIELDS

Bluefield, Bramwell, Greenville, Pipestem, Wolf Creek

About the region . . .

This region of the state is best known for coal mining, and its coal mining history. While the coal industry peaked in the region in the 1920s, it continues today, albeit using less manpower and more mechanized equipment. The town of **Bluefield** became the center of commerce during the area's heydey, and many of its venerable historic buildings can be viewed on a self-guided walking tour of the city. The town of Bluefield straddles the West Virginia-Virginia border, high in the Allegheny Mountains. Cool mountain breezes have given the town its nickname of "Nature's Air Conditioned City." Should the temperature hit above 90 degrees on your visit — a very uncommon occurrence — head to the Chamber of Commerce for free lemonade!

About a hundred years ago, the historic town of **Bramwell** became home to many of the region's coal barons. Hard hit by fire as well as the Depression, Bramwell still retains many of its more opulent homes. Several of the mansions are open to visitors, who will see extravagant fixtures and furnishings imported from Europe. While great fortunes were made in this region by a few, great numbers of men working in the mines suffered. Interest in the unrest in the region has been re-kindled by director John Sayles' award winning film, *Matewan*, which tells the story of the Matewan Massacre, in Mingo County. The entire region is steeped in Appalachian history, being home to many struggles of the United Mine Workers, as well as the legendary feud of the Hatfield and McCoy families.

BLUEFIELD

Dian-Lee House

The innkeeper at Dian-Lee House, Sandra Hancock, had admired the stately mansion at 2109 Jefferson Street for several years before she purchased it with an old family friend, Robert Dills. Mrs. Hancock picked the right friend for this project. Mr. Dills' resume includes his work at the Smithsonian and his serving as the design consultant for the refurbishment of many historic properties. Hancock and Dills quickly set out to restore the property to its former life of elegance, which had faded while the house spent several years as apartments and a boarding house.

Guests will enjoy the elegant formal rooms downstairs, noting an ocean liner's Art Deco bar in the study, an antique English pipe organ and baby grand in the entrance hall, and Louis XVI furniture in the drawing room. Hancock and Dills chose period wall coverings and fabrics, including the hallway paper, which was copied from a plantation in Natchez, Mississippi.

Upstairs the guest rooms are furnished with antique beds, family quilts, and amenities such as refrigerators and microwaves. There are four rooms with private baths, two with a shared bath, and one large loft apartment which has three beds and is suitable for a family or group of friends. All of the guest rooms have cable television and a telephone. Meals can be prepared in the guests' kitchenettes, and enjoyed on the adjoining sleeping porches and decks.

Private parties and dinners can be held downstairs. In nice weather, spend some time outside on the verandah porch swing. . . imagining a time period when things moved a little slower. If guests want to stretch their legs, there are jogging trails and biking trails nearby.

How to get there: From 460 West take the Washington Street exit. Go right at the stoplight, and take an immediate left onto Jefferson Street.

Innkeeper: Sandra Hancock

Address/Telephone: 2109 Jefferson Street, Bluefield, WV 24701, 304-327-6370/800-CALL WVA, fax 304-327-6410.

Web page: www.dianlee.com

E-mail: dian-lee@netlinkcorp.com

Rooms: 4 with private bath; 2 with shared bath; 1 large loft suite with bath. All guest rooms have cable television and telephone. Sorry, no pets or smoking. Children welcome.

Rates: $ 70 - 120.; includes continental breakfast. Minimum stay required. Corporate discounts available. Accept Visa, Mastercard, American Express and cash.

Open: Year around.

Facilities and activities: Guests enjoy the verandah and several decks in the summer; try a seat by the fireplace in the elegant drawing room in the winter. Nearby attractions include Exhibition Coal Mines, the East River Overlook, and jogging and biking in City Park.

BRAMWELL

Perry House Bed & Breakfast

Jim and Joyce Bishop invite you to travel to the Perry House Bed & Breakfast, and enjoy a leisurely visit. Located in historic Bramwell, seven miles from the town of Princeton, the Perry House was built in 1902. The house is on the National Register of Historic Structures, while the town of Bramwell is on the National Register of Historic Places. Bramwell was home to many early coal field developers in the first half of the century. Perry House was built and owned by the Perry family, who originally ran the bank in Bramwell. The Bishops are only the third owners of the house.

You'll find Perry House to be in original turn-of-the-century style, with only the bathrooms significantly altered. Visitors to the area can enjoy antique shopping, skiing at nearby Winterplace, and hiking and biking at Pinnacle and Pipestem State Parks. During the summer, guests can enjoy the talents of local musicians who frequently get together for jam sessions.

How to get there: Take I-77 to Princeton. Travel west on Route 460 past Andy Clark Ford. Take a right to the end of the street (2 blocks), and take left to a fork in the road. Go right on Airport Road, travel 3 miles to a traffic signal. Go right on Route 52 to Bramwell. Perry House is located on Main Street in Bramwell.

Innkeepers: Jim and Joyce Bishop

Address/Telephone: P. O. Box 248, Main Street, Bramwell, WV 24715-0248, 304-248-8145/800-328-0248.

Web page: www.holidayjunction.com/usa/wv/cwv0001.html

E-mail: perryhouse@netlinkcorp.com

Rooms: 4, which share 3 ½ baths; one room has a private bath. Sorry, no smoking, pets, or children under 14.

Rates: $ 55. - 85. per night. Includes continental breakfast. Discounts for AARP, ITC, Uncle Ben's Travel Club, and multi-night stays. Visa, Mastercard, and cash accepted.

Open: Year around.

Facilities and activities: The B & B has a working fireplace in the parlor, as well as cable television. The B & B is located near Pinnacle State Park, Pipestem State Park, skiing at Winterplace, and the Coal Heritage Trail and Exhibition Coal Mine.

GREENVILLE

Creekside

In the heart of rural Monroe County, nestled in a hidden valley, is Creekside. A charming group of cottages located on property beside the beautiful Indian Creek, Creekside is a wonderful place to restore the body and mind. A group of nine cottages range in style from turn-of-the-century to brand new. All are furnished with country antiques in a traditional B & B manner. Your host Natalie Sandell offers a wide variety of accommodations among these cottages. There are 2 basic categories of cottage: Deluxe Cottages and Couple and Family Cottages. Prices increase with the number of persons that can be accommodated in the cottage. Call or write for the extensive brochure which explains pricing: weekend, mid-week, and full week stays are priced differently. Each cottage has a fully equipped kitchen, linens, grills, firewood, bicycles, games, and radio/cassette players.

Deluxe Cottages: Our favorites were Creek House and Valley View. Creek House is a turn-of-the-century bungalow nestled close to Indian Creek. With room for six people, it has two fireplaces, a wraparound deck with jacuzzi, three bedrooms and two baths. Valley View has a deck with a large jacuzzi/spa and breathtaking views of the valley. It has six bedrooms, three baths, dining area, and a large living area with fireplace; it is suitable for 12 people. Each have a washer and dryer and private game area. Call for details on other deluxe cottages.

Couple and Family Cottages: Some of the cottages for 2-4 people include: Redbud in a private wooded setting, with an indoor jacuzzi tub, fireplace, complete kitchen, and private deck, offering a romantic atmosphere for two. Mountain View has a comfortable suite for four. The high deck has a spectacular mountain view from which to enjoy leisurely meals. Woodside is in a quiet woodland setting, with a deck, two bedrooms, one bath, and a fireplace; it is suitable for four people. Spruce Knoll is nestled in the woods, with a private deck and large jacuzzi, both of which encourage star gazing. It has two bedrooms, one bath and a fireplace. It is suitable for four people. These cottages have use of the central laundry, a picnic area with grill on Indian Creek, and an outdoor game area.

How to get there: Take I-77 South to Princeton. Exit on U.S. 460 East, continue to Rich Creek, go north on Route 219 to Route 122, Greenville Road. Travel 3 miles on Greenville Road, turn left on gravel road at Creekside sign.

Innkeeper: Natalie P. Sandell

Address/Telephone: P.O. Box 111, Greenville, WV 24945, 304-832-6433/800-691-6420.

Web page: http://wvweb.com/www/creekside.html

Rooms: 9 cottages. Children and pets welcome. No smoking inside. Weekend check out 11 a.m.

Rates: For weekends, deluxe cottages $ 460. - $ 690; couple/family cottages $ 155. - $ 345. No credit cards; accept personal check, cash, money order.

Open: March through November.

Facilities and activities: Outdoor pool, hiking and biking trails, jacuzzi, fishing, horseback riding, and playground.

PIPESTEM

Walnut Grove Inn Bed & Breakfast

For a year around getaway, visit the Walnut Grove Inn. Enjoy the beautiful fall foliage, try your hand at downhill or cross-country skiing, visit beautiful perennial flower gardens, and get wet at the nearby state parks. The Inn was originally a farmhouse built in the 1800s. On the grounds is an old family cemetery, where some Confederate soldiers are buried. The house itself is a converted log structure, with barn board siding and cedar shingles. The Inn is located on 38 beautiful acres, perfect for hiking, bird watching, or enjoying wildlife.

Guests can enjoy relaxing in rockers on the front porch or taking a swim in the pool. In the morning, enjoy the full gourmet breakfast for which the Inn is famous. Guests can choose from the following bedrooms: Victoria's Country Cottage Room with a king size brass bed; the English Rose Garden Room with two twin beds; Diantha's

French Boudoir Room with both a double and a twin size bed; and the Blue Rhapsody Room with a queen size bed and a private entrance. All bedrooms have a private bath.

How to get there: From I-77 take Exit 14. Follow signs to Pipestem State Park on Route 20 North. Go approximately 1.5 miles past the park entrance to Broadway Road. Turn beside Cook's Chapel and travel .8 mile. From I-64 take the Sandstone Exit and follow Route 20 South about 22 miles to Broadway Road. Turn beside Cook's Chapel and travel .8 mile.

Innkeepers: Bonnie and Larry Graham

Address/Telephone: HC 78, Box 260, Pipestem, WV 25979, 304-466-6119/800-701-1237.

Web page: wvweb.com/WALNUT_GROVE_INN

Rooms: 5, all with private baths. Sorry, no pets, smoking, or children under 12 years.

Rates: $ 60. - 75. per night; includes full gourmet breakfast. Accept Visa, Mastercard, American Express, Discover, cash and check.

Open: Year around.

Facilities and activities: Pool, lawn croquet, horseshoes, basketball, badminton, volleyball, and 38 acres for hiking and exploring. Available nearby are golf, horseback riding, tennis, archery, Sandstone Falls, Pipestem State Park, Winterplace skiing, and Bluestone Lake and Park.

WOLF CREEK

High Meadow Farm Lodge

For a truly unique and peaceful getaway, try High Meadow Farm Lodge in Wolf Creek, West Virginia. When a family or group comes to the Lodge, they are the only guests. The Lodge has eight beds of different sizes located in five different sleeping areas. The Lodge can readily accommodate 12 adults, and more if need be. Two small log cabins on the property are included with rental of the Lodge. For relaxing among incredible mountain views, there is a 500 square foot deck spanning the front of the Lodge. Many guests spend a good deal of time on the deck in the large hot tub spa. The Lodge has two full bathrooms, as well as a modern, outfitted kitchen, a dining area, and two wood stoves for chilly weather. There are hiking trails and a stocked fishing pond on the property, which is a 400 acre working farm.

If you grow tired of the deck and the hot tub, there are wonderful opportunities to enjoy the outdoors in the surrounding area. Nearby are both the New and Greenbrier Rivers, offering white water rafting and canoeing. The Greenbrier River Trail is perfect for mountain biking or hiking. For shopping and restaurants, visit nearby historic Lewisburg. National forests and state parks are also nearby, as well as several ski resorts. High Meadow is a retreat with a warm, rustic, and restful atmosphere that suits family vacations and reunions, executive retreats, or a sportsman's getaway.

How to get there: From Charleston, WV: take I-77 south to I-64 at Beckley. Travel east to Exit 161 at Alta; take Route 12 south to Alderson, cross the Greenbrier River and turn left after the bridge. Travel 6.4 miles to Wolf Creek, turn left on the secondary road 150 feet before the Wolf Creek Post Office. Go .5 mile to the lodge to check in. From Washington, D.C.: Take I-66 to I-81, south to I-64, then west on I-64 to exit 161. Take Route 12 south to Alderson, cross the Greenbrier River. Follow directions above.

Innkeepers: Tom and Ling Yu Edgar

Address/Telephone: General Delivery, Wolf Creek, WV 24993, 304-445-7684.

Web page: http://bestinns.net/usa/wv/highmeadow.html

E-mail: tedgar@brier.net

Rooms: One lodge which sleeps 12 - 14 persons, with 2 full baths. Also includes two small log cabins on the property. Children welcome; pets must stay outside. Check out is 10 a.m.

Rates: 2 day stay: $ 275. double occupancy;/$ 30. each additional guest; 3 days: $ 350./$ 26. additional guest; 7 days: $ 665./$ 22. additional guest. Children under 10 always free. Accept personal check or cash; no credit cards.

Open: Year around.

Facilities and activities: Large deck, hot tub, and beautiful surroundings. Sportsmen will enjoy the nearby New and Greenbrier Rivers, and the Greenbrier River Trail.

METRO VALLEY

Charleston, Glen Ferris, Milton

About the region . . .

Visitors to the **Charleston** area will not lack for activities in and around this riverside capital city. The two bed & breakfasts in Charleston – The Brass Pineapple and Historic Charleston B & B — both lie in the city's historic East End district. The East End is within easy walking distance of the state capitol and state museum, the Kanawha River, and downtown Charleston. In the spring, walk along the Kanawha, enjoying the profusion of daffodils and flowering crabapple trees on the riverbank. Downtown you'll find antique stores, boutiques, and restaurants. While on Capitol Street, enjoy ice cream, bagels, and cappucino, or shop for wine, fresh fruit and flowers at the Farmer's Market.

Leaving Charleston and heading east on Route 60, you'll travel the Historic Midland Trail. You may want to stop at the historic Craik-Patton House, Daniel Boone Park, or the small town of Malden. While in historic Malden, visit Cabin Creek Quilts and the TerraSalis Garden Center. Traveling further along Route 60, you will come to the historic Glen Ferris Inn in **Glen Ferris**, on the banks of the Kanawha

River near the Kanawha Falls. For more scenic beauty, stay on Route 60 East and visit Hawks Nest National Park. Take a ride on the sky tram and enjoy spectacular views of the New River Gorge.

To visit the **Milton** area, take I-64 West from Charleston. In Milton you can stay at the charming Cedar House. Another special attraction in Milton is the Blenko Glass Factory. Visitors can watch skilled glass blowers practice their art, and buy lovely wares in the shop. From Milton travel a short distance on I-64 West to reach the city of Huntington, on the banks of the Ohio River. Huntington is home to Marshall University, lovely Ritter Park, and the Huntington Museum of Art.

CHARLESTON

The Brass Pineapple

A trip to the Brass Pineapple is full of many unexpected pleasures, not the least of which is meeting its energetic and charming proprietress, Sue Pepper. The Inn's motto: "Elegant but Cozy; Our Goal: Your Comfort." The staff and amenities at the Brass Pineapple have been meeting that goal since 1993.

The original lot for the house was purchased in 1907 by real estate developer E. C. Bauer and his wife, Clara. The house was completed in 1910 using only the finest materials, including matched oak paneling, Italian tiles, and exquisite stained and leaded glass. Many of the windows are Tiffany windows original to the house; those in the dining room are especially spectacular. A special romantic detail is the lovebirds pictured in the stained glass window on the stairwell; it symbolized, as was customary for the time, the love of the original owners.

There are 5 bedrooms for guests, plus a bridal suite. All rooms are appointed with antiques, telephone, cable television and VCR, hair dryers, cozy bathrobes, and private baths. The room most popular with businessmen is the English Gentleman. It features an antique walnut bedroom suite with a queen size bed, exceptional walnut wainscoting, and marble baseboards. Likewise, the Victorian Rose is especially popular with many female visitors. It has an elegant, hand carved, queen size bed, and is decorated with roses and lace; its private bath has an antique claw foot tub. The Bauer Room, named for the builder of the house, has a high-backed, Victorian queen size bed made of walnut, and a private bath with a marble shower. The West Virginia Room celebrates the beauty and history of the state in elegant style. Guests enjoy its queen size, four-poster canopy bed and large, separate private bath with tub and shower. The room named My Grandmother's Room is a tribute to grandmothers everywhere. Its two extra long oak twin beds can combine to be a king size bed. The room is decorated with P. Buckley Moss collectible plates, and has a separate private bath with tub and shower. The Hearts & Flowers Bridal Suite is a deluxe private retreat, great for romantic couples as well as for individuals just wanting to treat themselves. Guests will enjoy the king size white iron bed, elegant fabrics, and entertainment center stocked with old movies. The suite includes a lovely sitting room and private bath with large shower.

The Brass Pineapple offers more than elegant antiques and luxurious guest rooms. The large staff consists of the owner, a full-time innkeeper, a housekeeper, and other part-time staff; they all emphasize personal service. For birthdays and anniversaries, they can fill special requests such as shopping for champagne and roses. They can also fully accommodate the corporate client. The rooms are equipped with a telephone, voice mail, computer desk, work light, and power strip. A fax for use by guests is located on the first floor. With sufficient notice, they will offer secretarial assistance, run errands, handle laundry and dry cleaning, and accommodate special diets. For those interested in a work-out, daily guest YWCA memberships are available, as well as bicycles for touring the historic district and downtown. For more exercise and fresh air, guests might enjoy a run or stroll along the nearby Kanawha River. For relaxing, sit among the ferns on the breezy front porch or under the forsythia and wisteria at tables out back. Parts of the rear terrace and balustrade came from the historic Holley Hotel, originally located several blocks away, but recently torn down.

Your hostess Sue also offers lodging at the nearby Benedict Haid Farm, as well as renting corporate apartments convenient to downtown Charleston. Because of its booming business clientele, The Brass Pineapple is often full during the week. Call ahead for a reservation.

How to get there: From I-79, I-77, and I-64, take Exit 99, go south on Greenbrier Street past the Capitol. Go right on Kanawha Boulevard, then right on Elizabeth Street, and right again on Virginia Street. Look for The Brass Pineapple sign on the right, mid-block.

Proprietress: Sue Pepper

Innkeeper: Cheryl Tincher

Address/Telephone: 1611 Virginia Street, East, Charleston, WV 25311, tel./fax 304-344-0748, 800-216-2123.

Web page: www.bbonline.com/wv/brasspineapple/

E-mail: pineapp104@aol.com

Rooms: 5, all with private bath; also have Bridal Suite. Sorry, no smoking, pets, or children under 12. Check out 11 a.m.

Rates: $ 79. - 115., includes full breakfast and afternoon tea. Two night minimum on weekends. Accept Mastercard, Visa, American Express, Diners Club, personal check, or cash.

Open: Year around.

Facilities and activities: Guests have access to voice mail, data jacks, computer tables, copier and fax. Nearby are the Capitol Complex, National Public Radio's *Mountain Stage*, the Cultural Center, historic downtown, sternwheeler cruises, antique shopping, seasonal fairs and festivals, and fine dining.

Historic Charleston Bed and Breakfast

Visit Bob and Jean Lambert at the Historic Charleston Bed and Breakfast. This is the second location for the B & B; the Lamberts originally opened the city's first bed and breakfast just two doors down. They moved into their current location, a French country-style home built in the 1920s, a few years ago. The house is a lovely gray stucco, with beautiful French doors in the two front rooms of the house. Not long after your arrival at Historic Charleston, you will undoubtedly meet BeeJee, the Lambert's Boston terrier. As you look around, you may enjoy seeing Jean's collection of Boston terrier figurines and collectibles.

The Lamberts' four guest rooms are at the top of a large staircase and off a wide upstairs landing. Three rooms have queen size beds, and one has a twin. All have private baths. The Bridal Suite has a lovely canopied bed and a large whirlpool bath. Breakfast is served in the large formal dining room. Jean likes to serve such specialties as egg souffle, blueberry pancakes, and strawberry waffles.

While staying in Charleston, the Lamberts will be happy to help you discover what the city has to offer, and give you directions to various sites. Reservations are recommended, especially during the holidays, but the Lamberts are always happy to help "weary travelers find a place like home."

How to get there: From I-77 north and south and I-64 west, take Exit 99, (the State Capitol exit), turn south on Greenbrier Street, go 3 short blocks and turn right onto Quarrier Street. Turn left at the first corner onto Elizabeth Street. Historic Charleston is the third house on the left.

Innkeepers: Bob & Jean Lambert

Address/Telephone: 110 Elizabeth Street, Charleston, WV 25311, 304-345-8156, fax 304-342-1572.

E-mail: bed2brkst@aol.com

Rooms: 4, all with private bath. Sorry, no pets or smoking. Call to inquire about children.

Rates: $ 65. - 95.; includes full breakfast. Accept Visa, Mastercard, American Express, check, and cash.

Open: Year around.

Facilities and activities: Whirlpool bath in bridal suite. Guests invited to use backyard deck area. B & B located in historic district near State Museum and Capitol. Within walking distance are the Kanawha River and downtown Charleston. Also nearby are Kanawha State Forest and Coonskin Park.

GLEN FERRIS

The Glen Ferris Inn

The lovely 150-year old Glen Ferris Inn picturesquely overlooks the cascading turbulence of the Kanawha Falls and the Kanawha River. On the National Register of Historic Places, the Inn served as house and home to both Union and Confederate soldiers during the War Between the States. Glen Ferris' well-tended gardens attract visitors throughout the year. The welcoming hosts of this Federal styled mansion beckon them to come inside.

The guest rooms of the Inn are decorated in keeping with the historical quality of the Inn. From Queen Anne to Victorian to Shaker, guests can choose from 15 guest rooms decorated in a variety of periods. Business guests may want to rent The Executive Suite. The suite offers a 6 person board room, as well as a wet bar, two baths, and a VCR. A second suite is also available with two large bedrooms and a common area overlooking the waterfall. During their stay, guests may enjoy browsing and reading in the wood-paneled parlor library.

Guests enjoy the Inn's dining room for breakfast, lunch, or dinner. You will feast on Black Angus beef and seafood, as well as traditional fried apples and yeast rolls. Dinners are by candlelight. The Inn often hosts wedding receptions, where an outdoor deck and tents in the garden are available, all along the riverbank. Across the street from the Inn is a new bookstore, complete with a coffee bar.

In nearby Beckley, travelers can shop at Tamarack, a facility highlighting the best of West Virginia craftspeople, including artwork, handmade glass, furniture and more.

How to get there: Easily accessible from Interstates 79, 77, and 64 to Charleston, WV. From Charleston, travel 42 miles east on U. S. Route 60. From Beckley, travel 40 miles north on U.S. Route 19 to U.S. Route 60 West at Hico, to the town of Glen Ferris.

Innkeeper: Natalie Phillips

Owners: Becky & Dan Hill

Address/Telephone: P. O. Box 128, Glen Ferris, WV 25090, 304-632-1111/800-924-6093, fax 304-632-0113.

Web page: www.emoney.net/glenferris/

Rooms: 8 with riverside view; 7 with mountainside view; plus 2 suites. All have private bath. Non-smoking rooms on first floor. Sorry, no pets. Children welcome.

Rates: Rooms are $ 60. - 75. per night; $ 130. for suites. Accept Visa, Mastercard, Discover, American Express, and Diners Club. Meals available in restaurant for additional charge.

Open: Year around.

Facilities and activities: Full restaurant, lovely grounds, gardens, and deck overlooking the river and falls; bookstore across the street.

MILTON

The Cedar House

Located on five acres overlooking the Milton countryside in Putnam County is The Cedar House. The Cedar House is a spacious ranch style home designed by your innkeeper, Carole Vickers. Carole looks forward to your visit, so she can make you feel at home. Trained as a home economist, she is more than qualified to ensure you have a wonderful visit. She invites you to relax in the evening with pool in the game room or by the fire in the family room. On warm evenings, enjoy horseshoes, badminton, croquet, or a leisurely walk.

When you wake she'll serve you a full breakfast either on the screened porch, in the privacy of your room, or in the dining room. Special dietary requests can be accommodated with advance notice. Light refreshments are available in the late afternoon, including home-made cookies and hand-dipped chocolates.

Visitors to Cedar House can choose from three guest rooms. The room with a king size bed has a private bath, television and VCR, telephone and private deck. The room with a queen size bed has a private bath, television, and telephone. The third room has a twin bed, private bath, television, and telephone.

How to get there: Milton is about halfway between Huntington and Charleston. From I-64, take Exit 28 and travel .25 mile to U.S. Route 60. Turn left (east) and go .4 mile (just past Mohr's Tire Farm). Turn left at the Trenol Road sign; travel .2 mile to the top of the hill. A gazebo marks the driveway entrance.

Innkeeper: Carole A. Vickers

Address/Telephone: 92 Trenol Heights, Milton, WV 25541, 304-743-5516.

Web page: www.bbonline.com/wv/cedarhouse

E-mail: vickersc@marshall.edu

Rooms: 3, all with private bath. Sorry, no children, pets, or smoking. Check out is 11 a.m.

Rates: $ 60. - 75. per night. Accept American Express, Discover, Mastercard, Visa, and personal check.

Open: All year.

Facilities and activities: On the premises enjoy a game room with pool table, family room with piano, guitars, keyboard and fireplace; 5 acres for exploring; central air conditioning. In the area visit the Blenko Glass Factory, the state's largest covered flea market, and the Mountaineer Opry House.

NORTHERN PANHANDLE

Sistersville, Wellsburg

About the region . . .

The Northern Panhandle of West Virginia is bordered on one side by the Ohio River, which has defined the transportation, industrial, and recreational opportunities of the region since colonial days. The states of Ohio and Pennsylvania border the region as well, allowing natives to cross the narrow panhandle from state to state as they work and play. Today it remains a region of mining and industry. This area is the most ethnically diverse region of West Virginia, thereby offering a wide variety of traditional festivals and eateries.

The largest city in the region, **Wheeling**, was once known as "The Gateway to the West," as settlers left the Virginias for new frontiers. Achieving its greatest prosperity as an industrial town in an earlier era, Wheeling still offers many cultural and historical attractions. The city boasts one of the highest concentrations of Victorian homes in the country, as well as a scenic riverbank and lovely parks. Oglebay Park offers lodging, golf, and a museum. However, the park is best known for its winter "Festival of Lights," which draws large crowds every Christmas season. **Sistersville** and **Wellsburg** are the home of two bed & breakfasts, and both towns are only a few short miles from Wheeling. Each September, Sistersville hosts the quirky West Virginia Oil & Gas Festival. For more information on the Northern Panhandle, call or write to: The Wheeling Convention and Visitors' Bureau, 1000 Boury Center, Wheeling, WV 26003, 800-828-3097/ 304-233-7709.

SISTERSVILLE

Wells Inn

A stone's throw from the mighty Ohio River, the historic Wells Inn is situated in the state's midsection, on its history-soaked western border. Ephraim Wells built the 34-room Inn in 1894 to serve the clamoring oil and gas wildcatters who spiked wells throughout the Ohio River Valley.

Like so many of their kindred spirits, current innkeepers Walker and Jody Boyd saved the Inn from a likely demise in 1994, when they purchased the hotel at auction. Walker is a retired chemical plant manager who just couldn't stomach the loss of an inn whose fine reputation was known for decades throughout West Virginia and Ohio. His quiet demeanor belies his energetic drive to preserve what is best about much of West Virginia — small town community life.

The proprietors work hard to offer quite a lot for a stay at Wells Inn. The Inn offers an off-site retreat called Next Farms, featuring a three-bedroom cottage with hiking and fishing on 640 acres. Extremely reasonable room rates include privileges at the Sistersville Country Club, a bucolic nine-hole golf course designed — surprisingly — by the legendary Sam Snead at the height of his professional career.

The full service restaurant, the Black Gold Room, features tasty fare three meals a day. Of special note are the fresh-baked goods, made on site. In the evening, after a fulfilling day trip down the river, relax in the Wooden Derrick Pub, where townspeople like to hang out as much as the relaxed guests of the Wells Inn.

How to get there: From the north, follow Ohio Route 7 to New Martinsville, WV. Cross to WV Route 2 south to Sistersville. From the south or west, take I-77. Take the exit to northern WV Route 2 to Sistersville.

Innkeepers: Walker and Jody Boyd

Address/Telephone: 316 Charles Street, Sistersville, WV 26175, 304-652-1312, fax 304-652-1354.

Web page: www.tylercounty.com (then click on "Tourism" and follow the link to the Inn)

Rooms: 35 business and period rooms with private baths. Smoking and non-smoking rooms available. Children welcome. Pets welcome with $ 10. additional fee per night.

Rates: $ 59. - 69. Group and commercial rates available. Accept Visa, Mastercard, Discover, personal check or cash.

Open: All year.

Facilities and activities: Rooms have cable television; a 1,200 title video collection is available for guests. Privileges at Next Farm Hunting and Fishing Retreat, Sistersville Country Club, pool, hot tub and exercise rooms. Conference facilities for up to 75. Sistersville sits astride the Ohio River and is the perfect starting point to visit the mid-Ohio River Valley riverboat towns, including nearby Parkersburg and the French-settled Marietta, Ohio. Each September the town hosts the quirky West Virginia Oil & Gas Festival.

WELLSBURG

Elmhurst Manor

Elmhurst Manor is a Greek Revival mansion listed on the National Register of Historic Places. The house was built by William Tarr in 1848. Elmhurst was constructed on the former site of Van Swearingen's Fort, which was built during the American Revolution for defense against Indian raids. One of Elmhurst's notable inhabitants was John Gabriel Jacob. Jacob was an anti-slavery Unionist, and instrumental in West Virginia's secession from Virginia during the Civil War. Many of his fiery opinions were penned at his desk in Elmhurst's main hall.

Guests at Elmhurst Manor will enjoy strolling the 3.5 acre property, often with the company of King Arthur the Great Dane, and Merlin, the bassett hound. The grounds are park-like, with a sea of dogwoods making a show in the spring. For sleeping, guests can choose the North Room or the South Room. The North Room has a queen size brass bed and antique furnishings. Complete with a working fireplace, the room also boasts heart-pine floors, high ceilings, and a private bath with tub and French shower. The South Room has a queen size mahogany canopy bed. It is also furnished with fine antiques and has a working fireplace. Its private bath has a lovely bull's eye window. Guests renting the South Room can also rent the connecting J.P. Room, furnished with a queen size sleigh bed and antique mission-style furniture.

Your hosts at Elmhurst, Carol and Bill Lynn, prepare sumptuous gourmet breakfasts on the weekends and all summer. Specialties include waffles topped with maple syrup and cinnamon apples, all circled with whipped cream. A full breakfast is offered during the week. Breakfast is served in the Music Room, with views of surrounding flowers, herbs, old dogwoods and towering oaks. Afternoon tea is served in the parlor in the summer and on weekends.

How to get there: From Wheeling, take Route 2 to Wellsburg. From Washington, take Route 844/27 to Wellsburg. Elmhurst Manor is located one block east of Route 2 on Pleasant Avenue between 16th and 17th Streets.

Innkeepers: Carol & Bill Lynn

Address/Telephone: 1606 Pleasant Avenue, Wellsburg, WV 26070, 304-737-366ï/800-584-8718.

Web page: http://168.216.219.18/hps/elmhurst.htm

E-mail: elmhurstbb@aol.com

Rooms: 2, each with private bath. Third room can be rented along with an adjoining room as a suite. No smoking or pets. Not equipped for small children.

Rates: $ 90. per night, double or single occupancy. Suite of two rooms rents for $ 145. Includes full gourmet breakfast on weekends and in the summer. During the week continental breakfast is served. No credit cards accepted, however business clients can be invoiced.

Open: Year around.

Facilities and activities: Enjoy the baby grand piano in the Music Room, or stroll the 3.5 acres of grounds. Nearby are Brooke Hills Park and Oglebay Park, golf, and Bethany and West Liberty Colleges. An hour away are horse racing, the Star Lake Amphitheater, downtown Pittsburgh and the Pittsburgh International Airport.

OHIO VALLEY

Parkersburg, Vienna

About the region . . .

The northern Ohio Valley is a charmingly rustic area, with the city of **Parkersburg** being the only town or city in the region with a population of over 15,000. While spending time in downtown Parkersburg, visit Point Park and board the sternwheeler heading to Blennerhasset Island. Hear the tragic story of the Blennerhasset's, and learn about their involvement with the infamous Aaron Burr, who reputedly brought about the Blennerhassett's downfall. Their Palladian-style mansion, which burned to the ground, has been re-built by the state based on archaeological information and excavation. Seven thousand square feet of opulence, the Blennerhasset Mansion is filled with antiques, oil paintings, and other treasures. For information on Parkersburg and the Ohio Valley region, write to the Visitors and Convention Bureau, 215 First Street, Parkersburg, WV 26101.

PARKERSBURG

Avery-Savage House

Originally built by the owner of Parkersburg Coal & Ice, the Avery-Savage House was opened as a B & B in 1996 by Sharon Mace and Tim Romine. Located in the George Avery Historic District, the house was built of masonry and stone, in the Queen Anne Style. It has a two and a half story hipped roof with several gables, a rounded turret, and a detailed wraparound verandah and balustrade. Recently described as "one of Parkersburg's finest homes, " in days past it was sometimes known as "Parkersburg's most prominent house of ill repute."

Decorated in antiques and reproductions, the Avery-Savage House will give you a true sense of the Victorian era. Guests will enjoy historic downtown Parkersburg, as well as nearby Marietta, which is a mecca of antique shops. Sharon and Tim have also added a hot tub out back for all guest to enjoy.

The Avery-Savage House has three guest rooms from which to choose. All three have both a queen size bed and a private bath. One of the rooms, which rents for an additional $ 10., has its own powder room. One guest wrote of his stay, "The hospitality, the food, the warmth were excellent. The trip back to the late 1800s was unforgettable. If we are ever within 100 miles of Parkersburg we will be back." Next time you're in the area, treat yourself to a stay at Avery-Savage House.

How to get there: From north, south, or east: Take Exit 176 on I-77, turn west on US 50 to downtown Parkersburg. (If coming east on Rt. 50, stay on Rt. 50). Rt. 50 becomes 7th Street inside city limits. Continue on 7th Street to Avery Street (eighth light). Turn right to first light (at 13th and Avery). Turn right on 13th Street, then right into the parking area. From west: Take US 50 to end. Turn left, then right to cross the river on Memorial Bridge. Once past toll booth, turn right (will merge with Garfield Avenue). Turn left at second light. Go through next light and up around to right. Turn left on 13th Street. Go through three stop lights; turn right into parking area immediately past 3rd light.

Innkeepers: Sharon Mace & Tim Romine

Address/Telephone: 420 13th Street, Parkersburg, WV 26101, 304-422-9820/800-315-7121, fax 304-485-1911.

Web Page: netassoc.net/averysavagehouse

E-mail: smace@netassoc.net

Rooms: 3, all with private bath. Sorry, no pets, smoking, or children under 14.

Rates: $ 65.- 80. per night. Full breakfast included. Corporate, government, and extended stay rates available. Accept Discover, Visa, Mastercard, American Express, check or cash.

Open: Year around.

Facilities and activities: Hosts can accommodate small dinner parties, receptions, and meetings. Parlor, formal dining room, flower garden and computer facilities are available for guests' use. Places of interest nearby include Fenton Glass Factory, Blennerhasett Island, Middleton Dolls, Henderson Hall, North Bend State Park, North Bend Rail Trail, and historic downtown Marietta.

VIENNA

Williams' House Bed & Breakfast

Bob and Barbara Williams invite you to visit their home filled with antiques and happy memories of a family now grown. Barbara Williams' motherly charm and delicious cooking will leave you wishing you were one of the children for whom the guest rooms are named.

The five guest rooms are named for the couple's grown children. Guests can choose from Gawgie and Pappy's Room (queen size bed, sitting area with TV, shower/bath); Rob's Room (king size bed, 2 twins and a rollaway bed, a television and VCR, bath with tub and shower); Connie's Room (queen size canopy bed, antiques, television, claw foot tub and shower); Bonnie's Room ("early acorn" high twin beds, antiques, television and bath); or Kay's Room (antique full size canopy bed and antiques).

Your stay here includes Barbara's delicious breakfasts, which are more than ample. Expect a full meal – and encouragement to have another helping — of bacon, sausage, ham with red-eye gravy, casseroles, apple rings, fluffy hot biscuits, or her special pecan-stuffed French toast. Stay long enough to have that second cup of freshly brewed coffee beside the pool or on one of the house's shady porches.

Williams' House is conveniently located in Vienna, easy to find and within a short drive of Grand Central Mall, numerous restaurants, Blennerhassett Island State Historical Park, Fenton Art Glass Factory, and historical attractions and antique shopping in nearby Marietta, Ohio.

How to get there: From I-77, take exit 179; travel south onto Route 68. Go 2.9 miles to the first stop light; turn right at the light. The B & B is located at the corner of Grand Central and 55th Street.

Innkeepers: Bob & Barbara Williams

Address/Telephone: 5406 Grand Central Avenue, Vienna, WV 26105, 304-295-7212.

E-mail: willhous@wirefire.com

Rooms: 5, 4 of which have a private bath. Sorry, no pets or smoking.

Rates: $ 55. single occupancy; $ 69. double; full breakfast included.

Accept Mastercard, Visa, check or cash.

Open: Year around.

Facilities and activities: On the premises, enjoy relaxing by the pool or on one of the wonderful porches. Your hostess usually has fresh baked goods and beverages for snacking. Stroll through the neighborhood or enjoy antiquing in the many local shops. Outdoor enthusiasts will enjoy the nearby North Bend Rail Trail for hiking or biking.

INDEX

NOT LISTED?

If you are the owner or proprietor of a bed & breakfast or inn in West Virginia, and would be interested in having your establishment appear in the next edition of *West Virginia Getaways*, **please contact Quarrier Press, 1416 Quarrier Street, Charleston, WV 25301.**